PERFORMANCE MANAGEMENT STRATEGY

JOHN LOK

ISBN 979-888591525-0

Contents

Foreword

Introduction

This book explains how different deparments can bring raising efficiency and improving performance benefits to every employees. This book include these chapters to explain how different HRM strategies can solve these organization challenges.

In chapter one, I shall explain what is human resource department role in nowadays business environment. What is HR's role in corporate social responsibility? What is human resource role in Hong Kong business environment ? Why does organization need reward management strategy? I shall indiate what is HM role in bank industy, hotel industy, auto mobile industry? How to choose learning or training method ? What are training and development steps ? What is HR's role in corporate social responsibility? Human resource role in Airline services: the demands of emotional labor of employment relationship between airline and airline staffs. HR role in business maximizing efficiency method etc. different issues concern HR role in any organizations.

In chapter two, I shall explain how good training and learning development department ,it can bring improving efficiency and improving performance benefits to any organizations' employee in possible, the whole HRM successful elements to explain whether it can still help the organization to raise employee efficiency and/or improve service performance, if the organization neglects to implement an effective human resource training course program to let whose employees to attempt to learn any work-related skills. I shall indicate one cause of marketing consultant organization teams need often spend overtime workload to cause finishing any projects after due date occurrence to influence inefficient marketing projects to give to their clients and bring negative emotion, due to it lacks good training and learning department to train their marketing creative skills to be improved in order to reduce the inefficient marketing projects issues occurrence.

In chapter three, I shall explain why and how one electronic assemble manufacturing and sale electronic products organization. Its supervisor and factory workers often work manufacture inefficiency and poor sale performance is due to they feel unfair compensation feeling because it is not achieve on manufacture performance increasing reward strategy and on sale bonus performance reward strategy to the shop supervisor and factory workers in this electonic assemble organization.

In chapter four , I shall explain how and why one efficient organizational development strategy can help the organization to expand as well as manage its employees more successful when it needs to expand its departments to increase employees number. I shall indicate this television broadcast organization why and how needs to expand and develop itself organization to increase many employees to work in different department and improve themselves skills. One efficient organizational development strategy is essential to achieve its organizational development aim in success.

In chapter five, I shall explain why and how one efficient performance management strategy can help bank organizations to raise or improve different department employees performance and service efficiencies as well as financial organizations employees sale performance.

In chapter six, I shall explain how to apply engagement strategy to solve one medical center complex and different cultural departments cooperation challenge in human resource management view.

This book is suitable to any readers have interest to learn different HR strategies to solve organizational behaviors challenges. It is suitable to human resource or organizational management or organizational behavioral subjects students to learn the essential HRM strategies how to solve any organizational challenges in business environment.

Prologue

CHAPTER ONE

Human Resource Role In Business Environment

● HR function in organization

HR role in business functions: HR ethics and code of industry includes that HR people should act legally, ethically and professionally as these aspects: Act legally, it represent the most core of obligations. HR is responsible for keeping current with changes in employment law and keeping management informed of risk or possible library. Act ethically, HR represents all employees at all levels of the organization, regardless of sex, age , race , color, material status, religion, disability or other protected class. At the same time, HR promotes the ethical culture of an organization. They must model the highest level of ethical behavior, administer all company policies and procedures fairly in handling disciplinary.

HR must conduct thorough investigations and make recommendations or decisions based on facts. Act professionally, HR must keep employees' and companies' information in the strictest confidence and protect company information when dealing with employees or individuals outside of company. HR must follow changes in employment law, company policies and employment issues. They are also responsible for continuing education to remain expects in the field to be a successful strategic business partner. HR staffs need own business knowledge and understand the cost of people-related activities and responsible for measurement to all HR programs and processes, subject matter expert, in this role, the HR person should passes HR knowledge in relation to the most up-to-date employment law at the best HR practices for sourcing and staffing, remuneration strategy and systems, performance management, employee relations, and people development and advice business as appropriate.

At all time, a professional HR will keep his/her management informed of any potential risk and liability to the business , due to the change of employment law. Creating good working environment, HR needs to motivate , engage, contribute good and happy working environment to le staffs to work in the organization. HR needs to help to establish and promote the organizational culture in which people are willing to do the best performance to the jobs, and commit customer's needs and concerns.

In this role, the HR person identifies and facilitates overall talent management strategies, employee development opportunities, employee assistance programs, long term incentive and effective communication opportunities and channels between management and employees. HR is such as one change agent. The HR person needs to know how to link changes to the strategic needs of the organization and being able to show empathy and concern employee needs to minimize employee dissatisfaction change. So, HR person needs have the ability to execute successful change strategies.

HR functions in organization include: workforce planning, sourcing staffing, organizational development, skills training , learning , talent development, reward management, compensation and benefits, employee relations, communication, engagement, HR policy and legal recommendation, change management, employee welfare, workplace health and safety.

Staffing sourcing means the success plan or buy recruit from external. It is a process , a company ensures that employees are recruited and developed to fill the key roles. Through high-performing employees, develop their knowledge, skills and capability and prepare them for advancement or promotion into even more challenging roles in 3 to 5 years' time. So, it asks to develop the employees to special projects, team leadership roles, internal and external movement to training and development opportunities.

The success plan should identify key position, its key roles and contributions, key success factors of key positions, skill, knowledge, capabilities, reasons cause of turnover, potential success identification, development plans for potential successor to reach the required success factors.

Recruit from external or buying recruiting resource from the labour market is suitable to meet company short-term staffing needs for the junior to middle level positions. It can help new skills and new experience. Sources of supply can be from a combination of full time/part time employees, recruitment agencies' temporary workers and contract workers.

The contracting applicants arrangement stage means the HR needs to contract the job applicants and invite for an interview, conducts the job interview, prepares the resume in advance and highlight areas to require further during the interview, knowledgeable about the company, the role in discussion and the job application process the applicants able to answer questions they might have, enthusiastic , friendly and courteous , so the applicant will be viewed the opportunity move positively, resourceful and helpful to hire managers , such as sharing tips ar interviewer, how to manage interviewees' expectation etc.

Arranging interview stage providing the shortlisted candidates with helpful information about the interview includes: when and where the interview, who will be in the interview, how the interview will be conducted. Facilitating effective interview, the interviewer needs to ensure the interviewing environment is comfortable one free no noise, not leave the candidate waiting for too long. When closing the interview, the interviewer should advise the candidate of the possible must steps, online screening of application forms, using online to search and compare job applicant's information, job skills, years of experience, education level to identify suitable candidates for further selection processes.

Reward management is concerned with the formulation and implementation of strategies and policies that aim to reward people fairly, equitably a fact, employers nowadays can hardly rely solely on base salary to attract and motivate their employees. More emphasis has other benefits , such as retirement benefits and learning opportunities. Performance and reward system should be market-based, equitable and cost-effective. Rewards do not only depend on skills, capabilities and experience of individuals, but also performance. In order to encourage top rate performers, employers must not only offer rewards for good work, but they must also have consequences for substandard work. Although, employers usually do not want to follow through with negative consequences, it is sometimes a necessary process. Otherwise, employees have no incentive to correct unacceptable behavior.

Employers also needs to clearly know about what is recognized by the company and how these will be measured. So that they understand the relationship of performance and reward. Total reward may include anything value resulting of employment relationship to the employee with a goal to attract, motivate and attract talent. It can include financial and non-financial rewards and that these can change over time depending on their personal circumstances. Employers need to find out what attracts, engages individuals and explore how best they can meet these needs. It is important that the company how design's the elements of the reward package to support.

What factors can determine rewarding for performance, qualification, experience, potential, behavior, effort, achieving goals, meeting targets. How the employees will be rewarded, the awards whether are company's work culture/characteristics are whether driven the right behavior/performance/efforts the awards are be valued by the employees, the awards are how often to be given, how often the rewards are reviewed, the award is long or short term.

Legal framework for reward system , such as payment of wage, restriction on wages deduction, minimum wage, benefit, such as share options or housing benefits. Major benefit plans may include: retirement benefit schemes, personal security, e.g. healthcare, dental , hospitalization, accident or life insurance, financial assistance, e.g. mortgage interest subsidies, rental subsidies, staff discount, education subsidies, personal needs, e.g. holidays and leave with pay child care, fitness and facilities, use of holiday house, employee shares purchase plan, company car etc. welfares.

● What is HR's role in corporate social responsibility?

The HR function should help formulate and achieve environmental and social goals when also balancing these objectives with traditional financial performance metrics. The HR function can serve as a partner in determining what is needed or what is possible in formulating corporate values.

At the same time, HR should play a key role in ensuring that employees implement the strategy consistently. For example, encouraging employees, through training and compensation to find ways to reduce the use of environmentally damaging chemicals in the products, assisting employees in identifying ways to recycle products that can be used for play grounds for children who do not have access to healthy places to play designing a company's HRM system to reflect equity development avoid well-being , thus contributing to the long-tem health.

How HR policies shape the workplace and how HR can improve employee well-being through better working conditions and more positive workplace a cultures. Top-management can encourage particularly supervisory support, also has been identified as key to employee environment actions.

In addition, adopting HRM and communicating a pro-environmental image can have a positive reputational effect. This helps to staff , the company leading to lower recruitment and training costs and a better financial bottom line. In fact, in some cases, a pro-environmental stance may be more important to potential employees. It can help a company address wider social problems that are affecting not only its external community, but also the company's financial bottom line. For example, The US postal service employees participate in more than 80 cross-functional teams across the US do drive energy reduction and resource conservation. These teams helped the postal service reduce energy, water, solid waste to landfills and petroleum fuel use as well as recycles more than 222000 tons of material. Thus, HR-related activities that can support , such as responsible workplaces, human rights, safety practices, labor standards, performance developments, diversity, employee compensation and more.

● Human resource role in Hong Kong business environment

Andy, W.C. el.(2002) indicated that economic downturn which began in early 1998 had dramatic effects on Hong Kong's prosperity and increasing rates of Gross Domestic Product, especially during the 1990s and the early years of the 21st century. In late 2002s, Hong Kong's unemployment rate stood at 7 per cent and showed no immediate prospect of diminishing. This has huge implication for human resource professionals and especially for their training, as managers of the organization's most precious resource, its people. Moreover, downsizing and consequent increases in the rate of unemployment were logical consequences of this process.

However, Hong Kong's strengths in finance, trade, services and tourism provided benefits from the effects of these recessionary forces. But, Hong Kong was faced with the poor of dealing with the human resource implications and other aspect of workforce reduction. Hence, it explains why HK organizations need to consider HRM functions as part of the acquisition, development , motivation and maintenance of human resources in order to bring direct relevance of the strategic decision-making on which profits and productivity depend.

Human resource management is focused on the development and application of policies in relation to human resource planning, recruitment, selection, placement, and termination, management education , training and career development, terms of employment and methods and standards of remuneration, working conditions and employee services, formal and informal communication and consultation through employer and employee representative at all levels, negotiation and implementation of agreements on wages and working conditions , as well as procedures for the avoidance and settlement of disputes and the creation of a fairer and more equitable workforce in which discrimination in any form is viewed as unethical behaviors.

HRM responsibilities include to conduct research into local wage levels to ensure the firm's reward system is competitive with those in other companies, devising remuneration systems to excite or encourage or persuade workers into enhanced effort and efficiency, administering superannuation schemes, e.g. retirement welfare plan, and advising employees about their pensions, maintaining personnel records and statistics, preparing accurate job descriptions and other retirement documentation, implementing health and safety regulations, accident prevention and the provision of first-aid facilities, e.g. safe construction site environment, designing and evaluating management training and development schemes linked with succession planning and developing and implementation systems with facilities organizational communication.

Role of HR manager includes the control function, such as analysis of key operational data in human resource areas of labor turnover, wage cost, absenteeism, monitoring of staff performance (staff appraisal) and recommending appropriate remedial action to managers; the advisory function offers expect advice on human resource policies and procedures, e.g. which employees are ready for promotion, who should attend a certain training course, arrangement contracts of employment, health and safety regulations etc. related human resource related issues.

The future role of HR manager needs to concern to adopt an international insight in their work, growing concern for the application of ethical approaches to human resource management, implementation of equal opportunity , data privacy, and arranging flexible working models, such as job sharing, job rotation, permanent part –time work, increased awareness to encourage or persuade for effective employee participation in company production systems in order to achieve raising efficiencies and effectiveness, concerning the consequences for HR management of the ageing workforce discussed issues, such as prolonging / shortening working age or shortening /prolonging retirement age policy, participating legal system in human resource issues, including laws on hiring , dismissing, equal opportunities, age, country discrimination conduct of industrial relations.

HR planning can help management in making decision in the following areas: recruitment. , avoidance of redundancies (increasing labor turnover, training, management and development, estimates of labor cost, productivity bargaining, raising effectiveness or efficiency , accommodation requirements. In order to achieve company's maximum benefits purpose, HR planning needs continuous readjustment (annual review) , because the goals of an organization are subject to change and its internal and external environment is uncertain. It is also complex because it involves to many independent variables, e.g. increasing skillful immigration job seeker number to compete in the country's local labor market or decreasing skillful labor, e.g. computer programmers, doctors, accountant, lawyers etc. occupation professionals sudden emigrate to other countries to seek jobs, consumer demand increases or decreases to the product. Hence , it must include feedback because if the plan can not be achieved, the objectives of the company will have to be modified so that they are feasible in human resource terms.

The human resource plan process to one company
is a cycle process. The first step may include that it
needs to follow issues from corporate plan's strategies and
objectives. The main points to be considered such as capital
equipment plans, reorganization, e.g. centralization or
decentralization, how to change in product or in
output, marketing plans and financial limitations.

   After it gathers the company's corporate
strategic plan data. Then, it will implement its
second step. This step may include three aspects:

● How to achieve the reasonable present utilization of human resources in particular: numbers of employees in various categories, estimation of labor turnover for each grade of employee and the analysis of labor effects of high or low turnover rates on the organization's performance, amount of overtime worked, amount of short time, appraisal of performance and the potential of present employees and general level of payment compared with that in other comparable firms. All these HR related data is essential to be recorded in accurate attitude.

● The external environment of the company analysis, such as recruitment position, population trends, local housing and transportation plans, government policies in education and retirement.

● The potential supply of labor analysis, such as effects of local emigration and immigration, effects of recruitment or redundancy in local firms, possibility of employing categories not now employed, for example outsource employees number, part time and semi-retired workers number and changes in productivity , working hours.

The final step is that HR planning needs to be achieved. It includes recruitment/redundancy program, training and development program, industrial relations policy and accommodation plan. The issues will appear in this plan, such as jobs which will appear, disappear or change, to what extent redeployment or retraining is possible, necessary changes at supervisory and management is possible, necessary changes and supervisory and management levels, training needs, arrangements for necessary and details of arrangements for handling any human problems arising from labor deficits or surpluses , e.g. early retirement or other natural wastage procedures. Following , it needs to give feedback , what will be possible modification to company objectives to company's corporate level to review its HR plan whether it can achieve company's objectives and strategic aims.

Human resource manager can be one human resource relation consultant to give recommendation how the organization should be better equipped to cope with the HR consequences of changed circumstances, careful consideration of likely future human resource requirements could lead the firm to discover new and improved ways surpluses might be avoided, it helps the firm to create and develop employee training and management succession program, some of the problems of managing change may be foreseen or consultations with affected groups and individuals can occur at an early stage in the change process and decision can be taken and by considering all the relevant , options, rather than being taken in crisis situations, management can assess critically the strengths and weaknesses of its labor force and HR policies, wasting or excess of effort among employees can be avoided and coordination to worker's efforts is improved to raise efficiencies and productive effectiveness.

● HR role in bank industry development

What is human resource (HR) role in organization? What factors can change to influence HR? They include workforce changes, globalization, ethics, organizational growth, increased accountability. These factors can influence HR's role change in the organization. So , when you assume be one HR manager, you need to concern : How have you used you awareness of internal and external changes to guide the decision making of your stakeholders ,e.g. discussing the impact of trends in workforce skills with function leaders? Which of your knowledge , skill, abilities or other characteristics have been useful in consulting with stakeholders?

Hence, HR role needs to understand the organizational goals and the role each function plays, serves of a cross-functional bridge. Locates talent throughout the global organization, identifies and supports need for resources or training, advices core functions on how with adapts to organizational strategy. Moreover, HR leaders need own knowledge of other business functions and whose organizations' business influences specific actions by HR , e.g. understanding the type of experts needed by R&D and future trends for that need. Also, the HR leader needs to know which of whose knowledge, skills, abilities or other characteristics have been useful in responding to this challenge?

HR also needs to consider how its organizational functions. They have disadvantages and advantages in order to achieve HR staff skill, talent to satisfy different departments' needs effectively and efficiently. Organizational structure has three types: Firstly, functional type advantages of easy to understand, specialization develop economies of scale, communication within function, career paths, fewer people and disadvantages of weak customer or product focus , potentially weak communication among function, hierarchical structure. Secondly, product type advantages of economies of scale, product team culture, product expertise and disadvantages of regional or local focus, more people, weak customer focus. Finally, geographic type advantages localization, quicker response time and disadvantages of fewer economic of scale, more people potential quality control.

HR also needs to concern when it's company needs to implement outsourcing employment need rea third party contractors' successful outsourcing depends on choosing the right activities to outsource, cooperation of contractor's performance objectives with strategic requirements.

Confirmation of contractors' reliability, capacity, expertise and ethical behavior. So , when the organization feel it needs to employ outsource contractors. The HR has responsibility to lead and know how to apply whose ethical practices competency in contracting for HR services or performing , due diligence or organizational sourcing, e.g. taking steps to protect employee data. The HR leader or manager also needs to know which of his/her knowledge skills, ability or other characteristics has been useful in responding to this challenge.

Standard chartered had have good talent management strategies to train its staffs. The talent management at standard chartered bank (SCB) features include: Standard chartered bank has good performance appraisal or measurement strategy. By making it a global standard to conduct face-to-face performance appraisals every six months. SCB is reviewing its own performance management objectives to make sure that those objectives stay relevant and achievable. Being sensitive to different cultures by employing different appraisal methods, also show that SCB understands the importance of managers and staff identifying and dealing with real, actual problems in a way that is most familiar and effective to them. Through appraisal, SCB also classifies their employees into 5 categories ranging from high potentials to critical resources, then to core contributors, followed by underachievers and finally underperformers. By identifying areas in which they are lacking and act.

What are the relevance HR problem to bring bank crisis to SCB. SCB view of employees as human capital in the organization, it could have at least minimized the less to a certain extent. For one, discussions between employers and still could have been more open and problem issues could have been identified at an earlier stage inefficiencies in the organization would have been uncovered , influence their performance against regional offices. In a way, having a certain amount of centralized control through talent management would also enable the monitoring of its offices globally. What are performance appraisal aims? Performance appraisal is the measurement of the effectiveness of an employee's job performance. The process is described as the collection and use of judgements, ratings, perceptions or more objectives sources of information to understand better the performance of a person, team, unit, business, process program in order to guide subsequent actions and decisions. The result or performance outcomes represent the contributions that an individual's job performance makers to an organization and its goals.

Performance appraisal focus on measuring or appraising the job performance of a individual, e.g. use of surveys or rating focus to assess and evaluate employee behavior. It brings the either positive or negative feedback to the employee in the performance view and the new goals for the next performance period may be discussed.

● HR role in India automobile industry

Human resource development (HRD) is the part of human resource management in any organizations. It deals with training employees in the organization when the industry feels it have need to upgrade skills to its staffs. It aims to let them to learn new skills distributing resources that are beneficial for the employee's task. For automobile industry in India example, India automobile sale companies will need effective HRD in their organizations if they expect to sell automobiles to global customers attractively.

Authors (May, June 2014) from internet essay indicated the India automobile sector is divided in four different sector which are as follow: two wheeler, which comprise of mopeds, scooters, motorcycles and electric two-wheelers passenger vehicles which include passenger cars, utility vehicles and multi-purpose vehicles, commercial vehicles that are light and material heavy vehicles and three wheelers that are passenger carriers and product carriers.

Why do India automobile sale companies need to concern HRD? Authors (May, June 2014) indicated the automobile industry is one of the key drivers that boost the economic growth to India. However, the year 2013-2014 has seen a decline in the industry's growth . High inflation , high interest rates, low consumer sentiment and rising fuel prices with economic slowdown and rising fuel reason for the downturn of the industry.

Except for the two wheelers, all other segments in the industry have been weakening. These is a negative impact on the automakers and dealers who offer high discounts in order to push sales. To match the decline in demand, automakers need good skillful of automakers to manufacturers attractive automobiles in order to attract foreign automobile buyers to choose to buy themselves any kinds of automobiles.

Despite the comprehensive market being under extreme burden, the luxury car market has observed a robust double digit like during the year 2013-2014, as a result of rewarding new launches at lower price points. Hence, foreign robust luxury cars competitors influence India automobiles sale number to be reduced. Hence, India automobile manufacturers felt automobile manufacturing workers' skills need to be train or improve in order to manufacture more comfortable and good design vehicles to satisfy future global automobile consumers' driving enjoyable needs.

In fact, India automobile industry employment opportunities will trend increase in the future with the number of vehicles available on the road today, the need and requirement for people who can fix these machines is fast increasing. The automobile jobs like automobile technician, car or bike mechanics are a great option. Becoming a diesel mechanic is also a significant alternative in India, auto labor market. Diesel mechanics are responsible for repairing and servicing diesel engines. As they are also required to repair engines of trucks and buses, other than cars. Even if communication with people instead of repairing cars in what interest to Indian, then Indian have opportunity of becoming a salesperson or sales manager in an automobile company. Career opportunities in automobile design, paint specialists, job on the assembly line and insurance of vehicles is also available.

Future India automobile industry employment trend is as the destination choice for design and manufacture of automobiles employers who need to automobile production skillful worker number will rise, because India manufacturing heavy vehicles, passenger vehicles, commercial vehicles automobile production skillful workers need number will rise.

Hence, India automobile sale employers will need have good human resource development model for the automobile companies, if they expect to raise automobile sale competitive effort in global automobile sale market. At the implementation level, India executives of the automobile companies need to strengthen their training, net working and more towards providing a satisfactory human resource development climate for its automobile industry car production, design, repair, salespeople employees and suggest suitable changes and corrections in the policy decisions for management of automobile companies and policy makers. Hence, future HRD practices in automobile industrial organizations for India automobile companies aim to identify the HRD mechanisms implemented in the selected automobile companies to achieve the training function to be effectively managed in the automobile companies in order to raise automobile sale competition effort in global automobile market.

● Challenge of HR management

As a HR specialist, what are the challenges you may face and what HR intervention mechanisms would you consider using in an attempt to drive individual and organizational performance in a multinational company? Critically evaluate this question by utilizing the appropriate academic literatures.

The challenges of the HR specialist when there engage in attempt of increasing the individual and organizational performances in Multinational

Companies through developing a set of HRM best practices, especially relating to employee recruitment and selection, performance management and staff retention. Since the organizations are multinational number of concerns are arises such as dealing cultural issues with the organizational goals as well as individual goals. Furthermore organizational behaviors and tools such as engagement, motivation and empowerment are basically highlighted; without those it is merely a dream to achieving the business goals. Basically Multinational companies are aiming profits and there for individual and organisational performance are very vital for their existence. HR has been organized in a different ways over the years. Some functions have emphasized delivery by location or by business structure. In these models an integrated HR team has serviced managers and employees at specific location or with in specific businesses units, with some more strategic or complex tasks reserved for the corporate center. The degree to which these different arms of HR were centralized or co-located and the question of whether they were managed by the business unit varied. Within the HR teams, depending up on their size their might have been specialization by work area (especially for industrial relations in the 1960s and 1970s) or by employee grade or group (responsibility, say, divided between those looking after clerical staff from those covering production) The advancement of personal management starts around end of the 19th century, when welfare officers came in to being.

There are some organizations where HR is seen as a central, corporate function with little advancement to business units. Some other organizations position themselves in the opposite direction, with a very small corporate center and all the activity distributed to business units. The question of best structure is how the function best organizes itself between the pulls of centralization and the pushes of decentralization.(The changing HR functions)

The HR assumptions and HR practices observed in high performing firms are the key elements to the formation of the Best Practice theory. Employment security, selective hiring, self managed teams, high pay contingent on company performance, extensive training, reduction of status difference, and sharing information are the key element of the theory. However less concern about the organisational goals and culture are given as draw backs for the theory.

According to the "best fit theory" a firms that follows a cost leadership strategy designs narrow jobs and provides little job security, whereas a company pursuing a differentiation strategy emphasizes training and development. In other words this argues that all SHRM activities must be consistent with each other and linked to the strategic objectives of the business. HRM uses various technologies to direct employees behavior towards objectives and tasks that deliver approved organisational performance. Many organizations try to frame these 'levers' with an overall performance management system, and attach incentives and rewards to achievements of objectives and targets within this. HR will need to reduce employment expenses to help organizations to save income. Direct costs include: Recruitment costs (advertising, admin, etc.),Induction/training costs, other admin costs associated with new hires, Overtime/ cost of temporary workers, reduced productivity cost etc. which are related to HR expenses.

In conclusion there is evidence to suggest that including the practice out line within this organisational behaviours and tools can used to drive organisational and individual performance in Multinational companies. It is essential to have suitable recruitment and selection process, performance Appraisal System and staff Retention plan to ensure the right people, In the right place, at the right time with right attitude. Training and development is also vital to improve HR performance. In addition HR Specialists role will be more specific when these techniques applying in to multi cultural environments where people perceptions and behavioral patterns are different from each other.

● The nature of the employment relationship

John, B. & Jeff, G. (6 edition, 2017) indicated Human resource management defines a distinctive approach to employment management, which seeks to achieve competitive advantage through the strategic deployment of a highly committed and capable workplace using an array of cultural, structural and personnel techniques. Also, human resource management is a strategic approach to managing employment relations which emphasizes that leveraging people's capabilities and commitment is critical to achieving sustainable competitive advantage or superior public services. This is accomplished through a distinctive set of integrated employment policies, program and practices in an organizational and societal context. Moreover, human resource management underscores the importance of people, only the " human factor" or labor can provide talent to generate value. It should draw attention to the notion of indetermination or uncertainty, which devices from the employment relationship:

Employees have a potential capacity to provide the added value desired by the employer. It also follows from this that human knowledge and skills are a strategic resource that needs investment and skillful management. Moreover, in the environmental change factor influences to any organizations need to provide a role for HRM in improving an organization's performance in terms of overall sustainability.

● What is the nature of the employment relationship ?

The nature of the social relationship between employers and the social relationship between employees and employer is an issues of central analytical importance to HRM. The employment relationship describes a relation between employees (non-managers and managers) and their employer. Through the employment contract, inequalities of power structure both economic exchange (wage or salary) and the nature and quality of the work performed whether it is routine or creative. They can be short-term, primarily but not economic exchange for a relatively well-defined set of duties and low commitment or they can be complex long-term relationships defined by a range of economic inducements and relative security of employment, given in return for a set of duties and a high commitment from the employee.

● Human resource role in Airline services: the demands of emotional labor of employment relationship between airline and airline staffs.

Positive emotion at work offers an apparent win to win situaton for airline organizations and individuals as it suggests that if a job or work is correctly designed, individuals will feel better and perform better. What was once a private act of emotion management is sold now as labor in the public contract jobs? What was once a privately negotiated rule of feeling or displaying is now set by th airline company's standard practices division. However, such as airline service waiter job, a private emotional system has been subordinated to commercial logic and it has been changed by whose airline employers.

● HR role in business maximizing efficiency method

John , H. (2013) described the work of police officers, we might discuss the functions of preventing come and catching criminals, the practices of patrolling, filling in report forms, breaking up disturbances, making arrests, and the qualities of commitment service. He also indicated police work is much more complicated than the brief suggestions and management work (including the management of police work) is much more complex still. It is hard to describe the functions without detailing the practices or to make sense of the practices without involving the functions.

John, H. (2013) defined characteristics of management is responsibility for an organization or organization unit and for the work of its members. The unit might be anything from a small retail outlet with one or two shop assistants to large corporation with tens or even hundreds of thousands of employees, but most managers are directly responsible for managing the organization of a manage number of people, typically between two and twenty and of the various processes in which they are engaged. So, we have sales managers and production managers and marketing managers and IT managers etc. organizing the work of specialists. The at the level, of the business unit or agency or regional subsidiary, we have general managers whose jobs is to organize and coordinate the work of different specialist groups.

● Maximizing efficiency method

Maximizing efficiency was a work study or time-and-motion to be exercise designed to calculate how the work could be most efficiently carried out. This involved the analysis of different possible divisions of different possible tasks of labour into specialized tasks. The optimization of the tools and machines, and the optimization of the physical movements, required to operate them, assuming workers well suited to the specified tasks concern. The optimized system would then be so as to become a standard requirement to be implemented with absolute regularity, so that the whole workplace operated as a machine. Workers would be selected with the skills and strengths to perform each specialised task, and trained to follow the standard procedures. They would be fairly paid for what was scientifically established to be a reasonable level of performance (assuming they were well pay introduced, to encourage over- performance and punish (underperformance). Both owners or employee would benefits.

It indicated conclusion was that output was determined less by working conditions or incentive systems than by the informed social pattern of the work group. Feeling mattered and wherever managers took a personal interest in the workers, made them feel important and generated mutually supportive and cooperative environment, output are enhanced management. It seems was not about mechanical optimization processes, but about leadership and team dynamics. The management characteristics were however critical and with some rearrangement they can be summarized as follows: A strong people orientation, every body is treated s part of the team and just as an replaceable resource, flexibility and teamwork value driven value system is through the company.

● six situation factors can influence management's choice of HR strategy

Beer , M., et al. (1984) explained that HRM and the issue of management goals and specific HR outcomes. The Harvard framework consists of six basic components as below:

Beer, M., et al. (1984) indicated these six situation factors can influence management's choice of HR strategy. Firstly, situation factors include workforce characteristics, business strategy and conditions, management philosophy, labor market, unions , task technology , laws and societal values. Any one of situation factor can influence management's choice of HR strategy. The situation factor can bring influences to other two components. Stakeholder interests component means shareholders, management, employee groups, government, community, union as well as human resource management policy choices component, it means employee influence, human resource flow, reward system and works systems. It emphasizes that management' decisions and actions in HR management can be fully appreciated only if it is recognized that they result from an interaction between constraints and choices will be influenced by situational factor component and share holder interests components and long-term consequences component influences.

The human resource management policy choices component will influence the human resource outcomes component, it includes commitment, competence, cost -effectiveness. It means that it needs to understand the importance of management's goals, the HR outcomes of high employee commitment and competence are linked to longer term effects on organizational effectiveness and societal well-being.

The assumptions are built into the framework are that employees have talents that are rarely fully utilized in the workplace and that they show a desire to experience growth through work. The, the human resource outcomes component will influence the long-term consequences component. It includes individual well-being, organizational effectiveness and societal well-being . The long-term consequences distinguish between three goals: individual , organizational and societal. At the level of the individual employee, the long-term HR outputs comprise the psychological rewards that workers receive in exchange for their effort. At the organizational level, increased effectiveness ensures the survival of the firm. The societal level, as a result of fully utilizing people at work, some of society's goals (for example, employment and growth are attained.

Finally, the sixth component is a feedback loop component, it is through which the outputs flow directly into the organization and to the stakeholders. However, long-term outputs can influence situational factors, stakeholder interests and HR management policy choices in cycle two way relationship.

● Knowledge management at hotel industry

Hotels' realization led to the design and implementation of a computerized knowledge library that was accessible to every site manager in every hotel across the Australia/South pacific/ South East Asia region. The system was designed to initiate a long-term knowledge-sharing culture by making it easier to share value-added practices and processes, thus reducing wastage of time and resources through replication.

The problem- The knowledge library operated as a two way system whereby managers could both add ideas or effective innovative practices and find solutions to some of their own operational problems that demanded new ideas or innovation. To simplify its use, the system was designed to store ideas by hotel function (that is food and beverage, housekeeping etc.) with both functional and key word search tools available , knowledge transfer was considered to have occurred once an idea had been implemented at another site.

Hotel management realized that they would need to create support systems to motivate sharing between the sites and geographical regions. This opened up an opportunity to achieve the desired knowledge, sharing actions and behaviors. Throughout the performance management system, as a result, for each site manager to pass their annual performance review, they had to retrieve a minimum of two ideas from the system and implement these in their hotel, as well as add two ideas to the system for others to be able to access and use.

The idea that the hotel different site managers' knowledge and expertise can play a strategic role in achieving competitive goals to expect to achieve a strategy results in superior performance, or a competitive advantage. Achieving high performance, improving employment skills, pay-for -performance, profit sharing, performance appraisal, team working, job evaluation, information-sharing, employment security, selective hiring, self-managed teams or team working, high pay contingent on company performance, extensive training, reduction in status differences, information sharing(knowledge management) benefits.

● Manpower planning role in business

Manpower planning (workforce planning) means personnel and HR managers need to ensure that necessary supply of people was forthcoming to allow targets to be met. In theory at least, a manpower plan could show how the demand for people and their skills within an organization could be balanced by supply. The idea of a balance between demand and supply reflects the influence of the language of classical labor economics, in which movement towards an " equilibrium" serves as an ideal.

The utilization, improvement and preservation of an organization's human resources. The four stages of the planning process may include: the first stage is an evaluation or appreciation of the existing manpower resources. The second stage is an estimation of the proportion of currently employed manpower resources that were likely to be within the firm by the forecast data. the third stage is an essential or forecast of labor requirements needed if the organization's overall objectives were to be achieved by the forecast date and the fourth stage, it needs to measure to ensure that the necessary resources were available as and when required that is the manpower plan.

There were two main reasons for companies to use manpower planning. To develop their business objectives and manning levels and to reduce the " unknown" factor. Firstly organization implements strategy and targets, it brings organization practices and methods, it brings manpower review and analysis (internal and external factors) , it brings forecast (demand and supply), it brings adjust to balance (recruit, retain and reduce).

Way of working includes: annualized hours, working time organized on the basis of the number of hours to be worked over a year rather than a week; it is usually used to fit in with peaks. Compresses hours, which allows individuals to work their total number of agreed hours over a shorter period. Flexi-time, employees have a choice about their actual working hours, usually outside certain agreed core times. Home working, either on a fully time basis or an a part time basis where employees divide their time between home and office. Job-sharing , which involves two people employed on a part time basis but, working together to cover a full time post. Shift-working , giving employers the scope to have their business open for longer periods than an 8 hour day. Staggered hours, employees can start and finish their day at different times. Term-time working, employees can take unpaid leave of absence during the school holidays.

● Recruitment, selection and talent management stages include:

Internal factors and external factors bring to workforce planning staffing needs options: internal via external brings to recruitment attraction via sources brings to applicant pool brings to selection assessment brings to job performance measurement brings to job analysis brings to workforce planning staffing needs opinions in cycle processing again.

Capable people who will apply for jobs within a organization. First, there is a need to attract people's interest in applying for employment. It implies that people have a choice about which organizations they wish to work for, even though during times of recession such choices might be limited. People may be capable of fulfilling a role in employment, but the extent to which this will be realized is not totally predictable. How capability is understood is increasingly determined by an organization's approach to talent management and development.

Under different labour market conditions, power in recruitment process will change between buyers and sellers of labour, the employers and employees respectively. Thus, in conditions of recession, employers are likely to reduce recruitment budgets and costs, paying more attention to developing the talent that has already been employed.

● Online recruitment

Budgetary factors will also affect how recruitment channels are used, with more use of online recruitment. For example, the ageing profile of the workforce around the world requires an adjustment of recruitment policies, the use of the internet and agencies for recruitment reflected to younger applicants, whereas older workers were more dependent on formal channels of recruitment, such as newspapers and journals. In addition, there have been many more graduates leaving university, and graduate employment is becoming very competitive. Many graduates will take longer to find employment that matches their skills. This might affect perceptions of the value to be gained from studying for a degree compared with the price of a degree.

There is a difference, however, in what recruiters think is important to this generation and what the generation itself thinks . Although HR policies will be designed to achieve particular organizational targets and goals, those policies will also provide an opportunity for individual needs and be satisfied . This view assumes that a fit between a person and the environment can be found so that their commitment and performance will be enhanced.

This an indication that the person to environment fit includes a person to organization fit, person to group fit and person to environment fit. If there is a match between the values within each of those areas expressed by the organization at the recruitment stage. The organization and the new recruits have a clear employees and can therefore manage those expectations.

HRM could help to shape the direction of change, influence culture and help bring about the mindset that would decide which strategic issues more considered. HR considerations, including the results of a review of the quantity and quality of people, the goals , objectives and targets whether they can achieve performance in an organization and for how work is organized into roles and jobs.

There has been a rapid growth in online recruitment , e-recruitment. As a result, organizations are advised to consider the design of websites and the terms that applicants might use to carry out job and vacancy searches. The usability of a company's website affects an applicant's perception of a job, with a focus on hyperlinks and text rather than graphic images and navigation links. However, issues with e-recruitment , including the one-way communication system, the fact that it is impersonal and passive, and the fact that it creates an artificial distance between the individual and the company.

● recruitment agent

However, once a recruitment strategy has been formed, an organization might outcomes its implementation to reduce costs and take advantage recruitment expertise, especial a large number of staff are recruitment. Recruitment agents act as "labor market inter-mediaties" between individual recruits and recruiting organizations. Financial service organization assessment and measurement of creating customer service performance indicators include as below:

Anticipating customer needs and planning accordingly, identifying the customers who will be of value to the company, recommending change to current ways of working that will improve customer service, arranging the collection of customer satisfaction data and acting on them. The analysis and definition of competencies should allow the identification and isolation of behavior that are distinct and are associated with competent or effective performance. On this assumption, the assessment of competencies is one means selecting employees.

Recruitment channels may include walk in, employee referrals, advertising, particularly online job boards, websites, labour market intermediaries, such as social media , social professional networks, recruitment agencies, educational associations, professional associations.

● job description

Job description includes job title, department, reponsible to , relationships, purpose of job/overall objectives, specific duties and responsibilities, physical and economic conditions as well as personnel specification includes physical characteristics, general intelligence, specific attitudes, interests, impact on other people, qualification and experience, abilities, motivation. Both job description and personnel specifications have been key elements, it replies too much on the analyst's subjective judgement in identifying the key aspects of a job and the qualities that related to successful performance.

● Selection

An organization wishes to recruit new employees to define criteria against which it can measure and assess applicants. Increasingly , such criteria are set in the form of competencies composed of behavioral characteristics and attitudes. Organizations have become increasingly aware of making good selection decisions, as selection involves a number of costs include: the cost of the selection process itself, including the use of various selection instruments, the future cost of training new staff , the cost of labor turnover if the selected staff are not retained.

There are good reasons why organizations need to consider the reaction of applicants to selection methods. If the selection is viewed as the attraction of the organization may be diminished, candidates who have a negative experience can dissuade others, a negative selection experience can impact on job acceptance , selection methods are covered by legislation and regulations relating to discrimination, mistreatment during selection will put off future applicants and may also stop applicants from buying the organization's products or using their services.

● role of HR technology

What is the role of technology in Human Resource Development? Identify some key forms of e-learning and critically evaluate their advantages and disadvantages, providing appropriate examples from organisations. It will define what Human Resource Development is and why it needs technology. Also it will discuss what electronic learning (e-learning) is, and will explain some key forms of e-learning and why we need to use e-learning. It will give a brief indication as to what technology actually is, and also the progression of technology. The essay will critically evaluate the advantages and disadvantages of using e-learning in Human Resource Development. There will be appropriate examples used to show

how different organisations use e-learning within their company/ organisation. Finally it will offer conclusions as to why I think technology should or should not be a part of Human Resource Development.

Why does HR development need technology?

Technology is always progressing and this is very good for companies who need or even sell technology. If we look at how a few years back within companies the secretary would need to file documents manually and this could take a long time, also apart from the time issue there were more serious problems like documents going missing or being damaged. This is where technology began to progress because there was a new technology progressing and this was the database and this could hold all the documents you needed safely onto the computer and that way it would be a lot faster and more secure for the secretary to file the documents. This is just one example there are many more ways in which technology has helped to progress companies. The example given here is just to show that technology is progressing and it will keep progressing much further in the future years to come.

Human Resource Development is all about learning, training, developing and education the employees in the workplace. There is a difference between these four concepts but there all correlated. If for example we looked at learning; this can be learnt anywhere and you can be learning yourself the new skills, but on the other hand if you looked at education you are being taught something but in a formal way but the two are linked because from both of these you are learning new skills and then you can go on to training and developing them skills.

HRD was not always known as this, there was a shift from welfare officers to HRD. HRD was initially set up for training and development and this was to help the employers in crafts such as electricians, or engineers as an example and from this they would be learning from their masters and will be developing their skills to be able to perform in the workplace. HRD created an integration of people management and development and this could become CIPD which stands for the chartered institute of personnel and development.

HRD likes to be strategic and is more for the organisation than the employees; it is also a long term method to help to build the company. HRD does like to implement change into their methods and this is why e-learning will be very convenient to help within organisations because it is constantly changing and this change would help employees improve on their learning and training and will be able to implement new skills within the workplace. Why does HR needs e-learning in organization? Firstly before I go into detail about how e-learning helps HRD perform you will need to know what e-learning actually is. E-learning used to be known as computer-based learning, this is basically what it still is, it is a way of learning but on a computer or even these days there is even m-learning which is through the mobile. We need e-learning in everyday life to be able to adapt the required skills in education, employment, even at home. It can be defined as any learning activity supported by information and communication technologies which is known as ICTs. There are arguments out there concerning the labels, an example of this is whether ICT-based learning is the same as e-learning, we can gather information from the world wide web channel and this would be our online materials, but we can also get materials from this intranet would could be confused as being from the world wide web but instead this material is delivered through an internal network of personal computers. E-learning is in fact taken to mean any form of electronic technology which can support learning this can be opposed to the chalk and blackboard technology which used to be the main form of learning.

● Why is HR strategy important to influence organizational success?
In organizational level, humans do formalize strategies as a function to direct and focus their efforts. However, in a business organizational (a firm), such efforts will focus on creating value for profit. In fact, the environment is a market with limited resources and therefore it causes competition exists. This environment mght be more or less stable, but it is in constant change.
HR Strategy will become a systemic and rational act, a process that can be managed in order to successfully attain in the golas of the firm. HR Strategy can divide these three kinds. Firstly, a HR plan is intended to achieve a particular purpose and to develop a HR strategy for dealing with unemployment. It is overall HR strategy to gain promotion. For government (public organization's economic HR strategy example. Secondly, it is the process of HR planning or putting a HR plan into operation in a skillful way. Finally, for war strategy, it is the skill of HR planning to be trained to the movements of armies in s battle or war. An example, of military HR training strategy, defend, strategies compare tactic.
However, nowadays, business organizations need " office of general", " command" , " generalship" skillful actions, leadership and leading welfare

from one leader, such as CEO who have any effective HR strategy to manage staffs and tasks as well as leading them to serve their organizations successfully. So, an effective HR strategy can give good HR planning direction to let the organization to know whether it ought need how to do in order to achieve its HR development goals successfully.

An effective HR planning direction can achieve the organizaton's HR allocation goals more easily. For example, knowing how it can use of common resources (e.g. available human and technological resources). A basic HR strategic advantage tool win and prevail over rivals in the market comes from the differentiated used of such resources.

In beverage competitive industry example, Coca-Cola soft drink organization example, it was still keeping its predominance in the beverage market product " Coke", Pepsi Co was advancing fast on the base of a successful "image" HR strategy targeting the youngest segment of the beverage market under the taste of the new generation. So, it can select to employ more young workers to work in its organization in order to persuade many youngest soft drink customers to believe it is one young soft drink health drinking company. By 1983, Pepsi had begun to outsell coke in supermarkets when coke maintained its edge only through soda vending machines and fast food restaurants. Although, different marketing strategic breakthrough by far unexpected. It follows all time successful formula of coke. In 1985, the " New Coke" was introduced after an extensive study of market trended, surveys, focus group and taste tests strategies. In these survey investigation process, it must need to employ many part time or full time questionnaires staffs, they can include students, housewives, freelance workers, unemployed workers. So, HR department needs have enough time to select the right applicants to finish the whole questionnaire investigation project efficiently and effectively. The HR arrangement need to gather information to conclude this goals, such as how to design the new formula (or taste) was based on a different (lower cost) source of sugar, high fructose corn syrup to replace cane sugar. All of Coca (the plant from which comes the allealoid cocain) derivates were also removed from the old formula. So, how to design the taste is the main survey information gathering aim. Also, how HR arrangement which can have enough questionnaire staffs to carry on gathering information from the taste tests in the limited time to achieve to finish the taste test questionnaire project efficiently and effectively.

What are HR strategic benefits? They include: It can assist an organization to protect its HR capital base. It is a well accepted business principle, it can also help the organization to extend this notion to the world' natural and human resources, it can help leaders to plan and measure HR employment and reward and welfare and performance management systems of business enterprises more accurately, it can help business leaders to do the best balance between narrow self-interest and actions takes for the good of unemployment or creating more opportunity solution benefit in society as well as they can do actions in pursuit of financial survival more easily.

Why can HR strategy help organizational change in success? Knowing the importance and implication of organizational change and admitting the fact that organizational change success and leader / leadership can play a key role in bringing and implementing these changes by deciding the desired form of an organization and taking the potential steps which are needed for the process. So, when one organization has one good HR strategy, it can assist its organization to change more people and non-people resources effectively and efficiently.

Why do organizations need to change HR strategy? Nowadays, dynamic business environments influence organizations that respond quickly and effectively to constant change. A dynamic enterprise has two important tasks. It must adapt the current business environment, e.g. people skillful shortage in the industry into a shared HR strategy and then quickly and effectively to employ talent people or potential people to do the skillful job for its organization.

Reference

Andy, W.C. and Barry, J. B. and Wai, M.M. (2002) , Managing human resource in Hong Kong, Hong Kong: Thomson, p.6

Source: The harvard model of HRM

Beer , M., specter, B., Lawrence, PR. and Mills, D. Q. (1984). managing human assets. New York: Free press.

John, B. & Jeff, G. (6 edition, 2017). Human resource management theory and practice, Palgrave, Macmillan publishers ltd. UK , London,pp.4-5

John, H. (2013) managment a very short introduction, Oxford university press, UK, pp.11-13

Sources

http://info.shine.com/industry/automobiles-auto-ancillaries/2.html retrieved on 14 th May 2014

https://www.kpmg.de/docs/auto-survey.pdf retrieved on 17 the June 2014

CHAPTER TWO

Training And Learning Development Strategy

What are the technique to training and learning deparment to solve which aspects of organizational behavioral problems?

John, A (2018) identified the major problems relate to HR personnel management, they include that selection of personal problem aspect, he explained that even if one knows precisely what qualities are required of man to do a given job well, it is still difficult to determine whether any given candidate has these qualities. On training problem aspect , he indicated that the cost of training staff is rapidly increasing, due largely to the increasing level of skill needed to operate modern equipment in the factory and office. Poor training will bring low earnings, high proportion of scrap production, mistakes, accidents results. Finally on salary and wage structure aspect, paid problems concern complaints of unfairness in the wage and salary differentials between levels of age, or skill, or between sections of the company.

What are the technique sector to solve above aspect of problems to HR? John, A (2018) explained that productivity bargaining, job evaluation, consultation and management by objectives techniques can be attempted to solve human relation problem; aptitude tests, intelligence tests, manpower planning, personality tests techniques can be attempted to solve selection of personal problem; needs analysis, programmed learning, business games techniques can be attempted to solve training problem; productive bargaining, job evaluation, merit rating, incentive schemes, salary progression curves, time span of discretion techniques can be attempted to solve salary and wage structure problem.

John, A(2018) , he explained that how to apply the aptitude test to solve selecting personal problem. He assumed that increasing technology needs an ever larger number of skilled and semi-skilled employees in almost every field of industry , e.g. machines and processes are more complex to operate and maintain, computers must be programmed. However , training employees to the new higher standards is expensive and it is becoming increasingly important to select any those who will be able to reach the necessary standard. One way to determine whether a candidate will satisfactorily complete his training to be test his aptitude for the proposed task before his/her training starts these kinds of aptitude tests as below:

The technique consists of analyzing the physical and mental skills required to perform the task successfully and then estimating each candidate's aptitude in these by means of special tests. Typical examples of the testable skills are: manual desterity, ability to understand complex progress for chemical plant operators, mental aptitude for system analysis. Also standard training tests are now available for estimating certain aptitudes and where exist little training is required to give a test to a candidate. The training test is often a highly specialized job. Usually it will be able of someone in the personnel department to use this training test technique, but executives should be aware of its existence. Aptitude test advantage concerns buying a standard test is low, but the cost of having are specially prepared by an expert can be high. The training required to use them and interpret the results is slight. For some of the standard tests the correlation between those failing the test and failing a achieve the necessary standard of skill after training is good, i.e. substantial savings in training costs can be made by unsuitable candidates before spending money on their training.

John, A(2018) explained that how to apply brainstorming technique to generate new ideas. He assumes that new products have appeared on the market an ever-increasing rate, that is to say many product life-cycles are declining. So, new ideas in advertising in display in production technique to HR development is needed . Many companies are finding that their employees think creatively. They begin to the problem is that most employees not only fail to think creativity, but tend to use the old product, old market , outlets, old methods and old equipment for as long as possible habitually. He indicated that brainstorming strategy is a way of promoting new ideas. The usual method is for six to fifteen people need to meet for half an hour and propose answer to a question from the session leader. The questions may be that how many ways, we could increase sales of product (x), how many new market , we can think for product (y), in what ways we can redesign product(z). Hence, each member needs to present and they can be drawn from all levels and from any departments in the company. The leader speaks his/her idea to let the every member to listen and no one is permitted to criticize this idea, his/her idea provokes member to think of another.

Eventually, several ideas may be developed into one that is entirely new. Only when the session has ended do they start the rational process of determining whether the ideas can be practices or not. Then, any promising ideas can be subjected to " reverse brainstorming" in which the question in how many ways might this idea fail? is asked. Hence, brainstorming technique is good training to let staffs to create new idea method.

John ,A (2018) explained that intelligence test can be applied to select the right man for the job. he assumed that this problem of one of the requisites for any job is a minimum level of intelligence. How can this be measured? He explained that intelligence tests intelligence tests consist usually of a long list of questions to be answers and problems to solved within a set time. The number of questions answered correctly within this time is an indication of IQ of the candidate. Some training is required to apply an intelligence test to a candidate and to interpret the results, even when the test used is one of the well known standard ones.

How to design a test of this sort is a highly specialised job. All personnel officers should know about this technique and in large companies it may be desirable to train one officer in their use. Its advantages include cost is low, it only takes an hour or to test one candidate or a group of them. The effort is hotly debated. Without doubt these tests accurately measure IQ is a large proportion of cases.. In particular they can indicate whether a candidate has a very high or very high or very low IQ , although some doubt exists as to their accuracy in the middle ranges. However, the real debate concerns the accuracy of the results so much as their value. For IQ is said to be a measure only of a certain type of intelligence and not a guide to other types which may be more relevant to industry. Psychologists would certainly agree that an IQ test must be supported by an impression formed of the candidates ability in other ways, such as at an interview.

John , A(2018) indicated that a clear job description is needed to define what each employee is to do. In some companies , the employees have not been told exactly what their job is, with the result that sometimes two people attend to the same task neither knowing whose responsibility it is, or some task is not carried out at all, each man believing that someone else is attending to it.

In large organizations this can lead to cause the company has intense frustration and annoyance to individual employees. The job description technique is simple, the supervisor writes a description of each job, specifying each major activity as accurately as possible and limitations. Very little training is requires, but obviously it is necessary for someone with a fairly detailed knowledge of the company to draw up such descriptions. This is usually done by the supervisor of the job cooperation with the present job. It needs seldom take more than half an hour of two people's time to write out a fairly comprehensive description of any job. It's content may include job title , tasks , authority, superior, committees, limitations.

John, A (2018) explained that job evaluation is one effective method to select the right rate of pay for each job. He assumes that the all levels of wage or salary earners is the differential in rate of pay or between one job and another. How much more should the driver of a bus get than the conductor, how much most should a crane driver get than a fork life driver, how much more should a manager get than a foreman?

The first step in job evaluation is to carry out a job description for on can not evaluate a job unless each of several headings according to the requirements of the job. Headings according to the requirements of the job. Headings used often include such aspect as: skill needed to carry out the job, possible effects of careless number of months experience required to each proficiency, working conditions, including any unpleasant circumstances, such as excessive, temperatures or dustiness. Each job is evaluated in this way and then arranged in order of ascending total points into financial terms. For example, the dockside crane driver, process plant operator, canteen cleaner job's maximum points possible may include headings of skill (10), effect of carelessness (20), experience required (10) and working conditions (10) , maximum points possible.

John , A (2018) explained joint consultation is the effective method to improve human relations. He assumes that a large company feels junior employees who feel that nothing they can do will have any effect, and the top management is indifference to them or their happiness. The result is sometimes indiscipline and always indifference towards the company, its products, its reputation, its managers. Joint consultation is one effective employee engagement method , which is one way of drawing junior employees into the company and making them feel part of it is to allow them or encourage them to participate in management decision making or at least to discuss with them the consequences of management decisions. Many of decisions that managers take are highly technical and need great skill, long experiences and the use of time very advanced management techniques, e.g. capital expenditure appraisal is on such area. However, many decisions are more of a moral nature or affect employees more than they affect the company. Thus, joint consultation advantage can make a systematic attempt to consult with the employees to seek their opinions, ideas, reactions.

● What are on-job training advantages?

On -the-job training means that having a person learn a job by actually performing it. Virtually every employee, from mailroom clerk to company president, gets some on-the job training when he/she joins a firm. It usually involves assigning new employees to experiences workers or supervisors who then do the actual training.

Coaching or understudy method means that the employee is trained by an experienced worker or the trainee's supervisor. At lower levels, trainees may acquire skills for, e.g. running a machine is observed by the supervisor. Top management level, to the position of assistant is often used to train and develop the company's future top managers.

Job rotation, in which an employee usually a management trainee, moves from job to job at planned schedule. Special assignments similarly, give lower-level executives firsthand, experience in working on actual problems. Its advantages include relatively inexpensive trainees learn when producing and there is no need for expensive off-job facilities like classrooms or programmed learning devices. The method also facilities learning , since trainees are learned by actually doing the job and get quick feedback about the correctness of their performances.

Stages in training needs analysis includes as below: Preparation , deciding the objectives and scope of the training needs analysis; data collection is from employees in the real world; data analysis is needed to analyze the training needs in a systematic way; recommendation to propose the training budget, training design and evaluation methods; action is needed to identify the responsible person and time frame, and implement the plan,

Training principle means the effective motivation of the trainee is needed by the design of the training program and the methods which are used, the designing a training course is needed to consider the training requirements: attitudes, skills, knowledge. For example, a shop assistant in a convenience store, would require a certain friendly service attitude towards customers, skill in selling, displaying arrangement and knowledge of stock, sale procedures and the company's general policy.

On -the -job-training is given in the normal work situation, the trainee needs to use the actual tools, equipment, document, or materials, that he/she will use when fully trained. The trainee is regarded as a partly productive worker from the time training begins. Off-the-job training is taken away from the normal work situation, usually employing specially simplified tools and equipment. The trainee is not regarded as a productive worker from the beginning, it is exercise practice. Off-the-job training is needed to implement on the company's premises at a training center or at an educational institution.

On-the -job training advantages include that it is less costly because it uses normal equipment, the trainee is proficient, there is no transfer of learning problems, the trainee is in the production environment, he/she does not need to adjust to it after the less realistic conditions. Its disadvantages include the trainee may be a poor teacher and may not have enough time to give proper training, if there is a payment-by-results scheme, if may discourage the trainer from training, the training may be implemented in an inefficient way, a large amount of spoiled work and scrap material may be produced, valuable equipment may be damaged, the production conditions, which are stressful, i.e. noisy, busy, confusing, stress of this type usually inhibits learning. Otherwise, off-job-training advantages include the training is given by a specialist trainer and it should be of higher quality, special equipment, simplified of necessary can be used, the trainee can learn the job from easy to difficulty in planned stage, it is fee pressure of payment-by-work scheme, noise, danger, publicity, the trainee will learn correct methods from the beginning, the trainee does not damage valuable equipment or produce spoiled work or scrap, it is easier to calculate the cost of off-the -job training because it is more self contained. It's disadvantages include the higher costs of separate premises, equipment and trainers, learning difficulties to the trainee, when he/she needs to change training equipment to production equipment and a classroom environment to a production environment.

● The four steps of learning requirement

Any learning requirement include four steps: identifying the problem, seeking a solution, selecting an applying training and setting objectives. In seeking solutions steps, common performance problems and solutions include: lacks of skill problem can be solved to provide suitable skill training, insufficient knowledge problem can be solved by training to broaden understanding, lack of motivation problem can be solved by training might-enthuse, attitude problems can be solved by training of management commitment.

The important concern is that the training's topics and contents need to achieve this aim to improve employee (trainee) individual behavior, such as improvement of efficiency is concerned primary with doing things right, when effectiveness is about doing the right things well. Because highly efficient training courses do not mean that the training courses and contents are effective relevant to the company or individuals concerned needs.

Why does training need to set objectives? Because it can let the trainer gins a better understanding of the desired behaviors when it is seeking to encourage to achieve the training efficiently and effectively, let participants to know what the course details will help to overcome any uncertainty, and assist in motivating the individual and training objectives can indicate what the needs and requirements of the company. It can reduce the waste a quantifiable return on the time and capital invested before it has clear objectives for the training achievement.

Why does know what the main objective for training is more important? It has difference between aims and objectives. Aims mean to provide a direction or statement of intent. So, aim is at target, but the objective could be more clear. Whether this objective is realistic one would depend on the people involved and the circumstances under which they operate. This means that when an aim might express a desired outcome, it is the objective which will seek how and when this is attained or desired more easily. So, when the trainer can predict what (are) is the more accurate objective(s) , when this objective(s) is (are) confirmed the real need to the organization's benefit. The training will be more effective or avoids ineffective training consequence (irrelevant training courses and contents) to let trainees (participants) to learn, it means that time and money wasting of the training course.

David, L. (2016) explained that why a lesson plan is necessary. He indicated that " the existence of lesson plan can have positive effects. It depends on whether the methodology of knowledge (the how we do it) , but at this stage we are simply examining the knowledge itself (what knowledge are we trying to communicate). However, there are three principle classifications of information. Firstly information that the group must know, it means that there are items of information which are essential to the understanding of the topic in question. In most cases, they will have already been identified in any training need analysis and as they are fundamental to the success of any training course on the subject they must be given the highest priority. Secondly, information which trainers should know would include anything which related directly to the information in the must show category. For example, this might include other practices and procedures which interlink with those requires for safety reasons. Finally, the could know matters are those which can be described as useful to the group , but largely incident to the subject. These are items of information which , if time permits, could provide a useful background to the topic , but won't directly assist in its effective execution. This category would include historical details, boarder aspects, of the task, further areas of interest and general information."

The classification of information into these three categories allows each aspect of the subject to be examined and assigned to the appropriate category. In this way, it is possible to provide a degree of prioritization , enabling all the essential elements to be concerned in time available and any secondary information to be incorporated as and when circumstances permit.

However, these are number of other factors which will have an impact upon the structure topic and content of any training course . These include: level of understanding, course size, availability of equipment and material, financial constraints and timing. For example, a person's existing knowledge or cognitive inventory will influence whose level of understanding whether it is more or less easily when the trainee is learning the training course, the number of people participation will affect how much can be accomplished and what facilities and trainers are necessary for the course size arrangement, the availability of equipment and materials, e.g. what materials are needed and are available to avoid the kinds of equipment limited supply shortage, the financial constraints' aim to satisfy the course objectives at the lowest cost feasible, and achieve the highest standard of training possible at a cost that is acceptable to the organization. If the objectives of the course can't be achieved within the limits of available budget, then it is better not to run the course at all then to run unsuccessfully. Finally, the training course whether it has enough time to prepare all teaching arrangement to avoid bad or ineffective training consequence and not to cover-estimate what can accomplished during this period.

● Training and development steps

Gary, D. (2000) indicated that employee orientation provides new employees with basic background information, who need to perform their jobs satisfactorily , such as information about company rules. Orientation is actually part of the employer's new employee socialization process. Socialization is the ongoing process of researching in all employee the attitudes, standards, values, and patterns of behavior that are expected by the organization and its departments.

Training refers to the methods used to give new or present employees the skills, they need to perform their jobs. Training might mean showing how to operate its new methods, a new supervisor how to interview and appraise employees. Training is used to focus mostly on teaching technical skills, such as teachers devises lesson plans. However, technical training likes that is no longer sufficient. Employers have had to adapt to rapid technological changes, improve product and service quality and boost productivity to stay competitive. Improving quality (quality improvement programs) require employee who can produce charts and graphs and analyze data. Similarly, employees need skills (training) in team building, decision making, and communication, as well as technological and computer skills (such as desktop publishing, computer aided design and manufacturing) . And as competition demands better service, employees require customer service training for the tools and abilities require to serve customers.

Gary, D. (2000) also explains the five step training and development process, such as below:

First step is needs analysis, which identifies specific job performance skills needed to improve performance and productivity, analysing the audience to ensure that the program will be suited to their specific levels of education , experience and skills as well as their attitudes and personal motivations, using research to develop specific measurable knowledge and performance objectives.

Second step is instructional design, which gathers instructional objectives, methods, media description of and sequence of content examples, exercises and activities. Organizing them into a curriculum that supports adult learning theory and provides a blueprint for program development. Making sure all materials, such as video scripts, leaders' guides, and participants' work tools, complement each other are written clearly into the started learning objectives, carefully and professional handle all program elements, whether reproduced on paper, film or tape to ensure quality and effectiveness.

Third step is validation, which introduces and validates the training before a representative audience. Base final revisions on pilot results to ensure program effectiveness.

Fourth step is implementation, when applicable , boost success with a train-the-trainer workshop that focuses on presentation knowledge and skills in addition to training content.

Fifth step is evaluation and follow up, assess program success according to: reaction to document that learners' immediate reactions to the training, learning to use feedback devices or pre to measure what learners have actually learned, behavior to note supervisors' reactions to learners' performance following completion of the training. This is one way to measure the degree to which learners apply new skills and knowledge to their jobs, result to determine the level of improvement in job performance and assess needed maintenance.

● How to choose learning or training method

Methods of learning, training and development plans, training sources can be internal to the company or employees are trained from an external organization. Training can range from short term to long term, from online to in-person and from low cost to high cost development program for senior or specialist staff could learn techniques , such as coaching and mentoring or second, formal or off-the-job learning or educational arrangement.

The choice of learning methods depend on several factors include: the nature and degree of priority of the learning needs, type of occupation, level of seniority and qualifications/educational background of learners, organizational culture, evaluation of the effectiveness of previous learning and training results, experience, time required to complete training, learner preference, each individual may prefer learning in different ways, some prefer classroom learning over real-life practicing , learner preference's over learning ways and styles and their individual characteristics need to be taken into account when selecting , developing and delivering learning methods. For example, in-house courses provide an opportunity to focus on company specific issues. External courses involves interaction with people from other companies. For example, in-house, on the job training aims to deliver on a one-to-one basis at the trainee's place of work, allocated time to a specified , planned and structured activity.

Reference

David , L. (3 edition, 2016). The Group Trainer's Handbook, Designing And Delivering Training For groups , Kogan Page , US pp. 18-19
Gary, D. (8 edition, 2000), Human resource management , Prentice hall, New Jersey.pp. 248-251
John, A. (2018) Management techniques, a practical guide, London, UK and New York , US: Routledge, pp. 27, 34-37, 67, 70-71,133, 140-144.

● Training And Learning Development solves marketing consultant organization time pressure problem case

Will this long time pressure to overload project finishing after due date to any marketing team work project finishing problem avoid if this marketing consultant organization had one training and learning development to train every marketing members' to raise creaive ability to know how to apply marketing knowledge to cooperate to work together to finish any marketing project efficiently and effectively ? Ought this marketing consultant organization need to reduce time pressure to let marketing consultants to cooperate to finish any marketing research projects before due date more easily?

This cause explains that one successful training and learning deparment can help any organizations to solve members cooperation challenge as well as raising team work efficiency in possible. Describe people related problems or issues, one marketing consultant firm, Ann Wood faced personnel problem during the day. Ann Wood, marketing director faced problem of two senior marketing analysts would leave her marketing research department as well as after these two senior market analysts left her department, it would cause the one urgent and important market analysis was delayed and it was more difficult to finish before the due date. Ann Wood, her marketing research manager, Joe would lack these two senior market analysts continue to assist whose marketing department to help to finish this one important market analysis during the date. The result of the one important market analysis was delayed to finish after the due date. Ann Wood would face her employer felt who could not achieve excellent performance to promote to do this marketing director position to manage her marketing research department to operate successfully. Even, after these two senior marketing analysists decided to leave Ann, marketing director her marketing department during the day. This issue would influence the overall many teams of other marketing analysts and senior marketing analysts who lost more confidence to serve Ann Wood's marketing department to cause it would have many marketing analysts and senior marketing analysts would plan to leave her department after her first working day. However, the major factor caused these two senior marketing analysts decided to leave her department during the day, it is possible that because their office computers were broken down, so they could not use internet to send this important marketing analysis project to let their manager and Ann, marketing director to read by email during the day or they felt their salaries level were below than marketing salary level, so they had planned to leave during Ann wood her first work day . During the day, the reasons of these two senior marketing analysts who planned leaving include that they felt who were very talented in whose job and had won several key projects as proof, so who ought earn higher salary, During the day, after their leaving, some other marketing analysts also planned to leave because who felt these two senior marketing analysts leaving, then they would rise workloads rapidly and they felt the marketing salaries level were higher than their current salaries unfairly. Hence, Ann Wood would face some marketing analysts and senior marketing analysts would leave her department during the day.

Suggestion of time pressure reducing method

Did the marketing consultant can handle to finish any marketing research project in team effectively before due date, when she feel to work in one reducing time pressure working environment?

I think she did not handle effectively in these people related matters. An effective senior manager needs to spend much time talking with insiders and outsiders about vision, strategy, and other major issues to the direction of the organization. A senior leader needs to make the strategic decision for the firm. Skills in conceptualizing, communicating and understanding the perspectives of others are critical for these discussion. A senior manager also needs spend time helping middle managers to define and redefine their roles and to manage conflict because middle managers are often central to the organization's communication networks. Skills in listening, conflict management, negotiating and motivating are important for these activities. Ann Wood ought attempt to use these methods to handle her staffs personal problems effectively.

Engagement is as the extent to which staffs enjoy and believe in what who do and feel valued for doing it. So, if they feel enjoyment, her staffs tend to receive more pleasure and satisfaction from what who do if who are in jobs or roles that match both their interests and skills. For example, some people like jobs that require travel enjoyment, when some prefer not to travel. Others like a high risk/high reward bonus plan where others prefer a more stable and predictable salary. Some individuals like work in a team environment, others like work more independently. So, Ann Wood (head of marketing) can make questionnaires to enquire every project team members what non financial and financial rewards are who want to get from this employer in order to raise their efficiency to work and reduce the leaving staff numbers in every project team.

In belief, if her staffs felt who were making meaningful contributions to their jobs, their current employer and society. Then, who should tend to be more engaged to the connection between what every project team does every day and the goals and mission of Ann Wood's company can be engaged successfully. Other people related problem is Ann's staffs lack enough marketing research skill and working experience. For example, Ann's one of staff Joe Jackson, the current manager of the market research group, who complained to Ann about the company's intranet had been down about half of the night and this technical problem had prevented timely access to data from a central server, resulting in a delay in the completion of an important market analysis on her first work day. He could not attempt to find any department staffs to help him to solve this problem. He did not know that whose some marketing research projects should delay if who waited Ann arrived office and then enquired her how to solve. Moreover, every marketing team members who ought lack enough marketing research working skills because who have no anyone could have confidence to finish every important and urgent marketing research projects before due date. Otherwise, if they had specialised marketing research skill, they ought spend little time to finish these urgent and important projects. So, the computer technical problem would not influence their projects to be finish. Thus Ann would face that many staffs will leave her department and the important and urgent marketing research projects will be delayed to finish after the due date.

What do I believe she should have done when she feels that she is working in one time pressure reducing working environment?

On the one hand, Ann only believed Joe, the current manager of the market research group whose suggestions to increase the market analysts salary if she want to increase their speed to finish every marketing research analysis and reducing the market analysts turnover numbers. She had not enquire other different marketing research managers idea why they could not finish every marketing research project quickly. What the problems were caused who are encountered to finish every marketing research project slowly.

On the other hand, Ann could not know what the urgent jobs are who ought need to solve. When Joe, the current manager of the market research group told her that the company's intranet has been broken to cause a delay in the completion of an important market analysis. After she had not attempted to find the computer technical staffs to help her to repair intranet during the day and she still to read any email in her office computer during the day.

I think Ann needed to attempt to find computer technical staffs to help her to repair intranet immediately and she ought not spend much time to see email, she ought continue enquire whether intranet had been repaired and the completion of an important market analysis had been sent during the day and she ought not spend much time to discuss to increase salaries matter to market analysts with Joe during the day. Thus, Ann did not know what the duties are needed to handle urgently during the day effectively.

Is Ann Wood a high involvement manager, due to Ann often feel time pressure to work? provide evidence.

I feel that Ann Wood is not a high involvement manager. From the motivational and leadership practices of managers to the internal dynamic of employee-based teams to the values that provide the base for the organization's culture, successful firms develop approaches that unleash the potential of their people (human capital). However, Ann Wood does not understand the actions of every team individual member and every team group in her marketing research department as well as who also does not understand the actions focused on acquiring, developing, and applying the knowledge and skills of every team members as well as who lacks an approach that involved organizing and managing every team's knowledge and skill effectively

to implement her marketing research department's strategy and gains a competitive advantage. Thus, if Ann, head of marketing director could organize and manage every marketing research team effectively, the knowledge and skills of every marketing research team member in the marketing research department can drive sustainable competitive advantages and long term financial success. For example, Ann's one of staff Joe Jackson, the current manager of the market research group, who complained to Ann about the company's intranet had been down about half of the night and this technical problem had prevented timely access to data from a central server, resulting in a delay in the completion of an important market analysis on her first work day. He could not attempt to find any department staffs to help him to solve this problem. He did not know that whose some marketing research projects should delay if who waited Ann arrived office and then enquired her how to solve. Moreover, every marketing team members who ought lack enough marketing research working skills because who have no anyone could have confidence to finish every important and urgent marketing research projects before due date. Otherwise, if they had specialised marketing research skill, they ought spend little time to finish these urgent and important projects. So, the computer technical problem would not influence their projects to be finish. I think she did not handle effectively in these people related matters.

An effective senior manager needs to spend much time talking with insiders and outsiders about vision, strategy, and other major issues to the direction of the organization. A senior leader needs to make the strategic decision for the firm. Skills in conceptualizing, communicating and understanding the perspectives of others are critical for these discussion. A senior manager also needs spend time helping middle managers to define and redefine their roles and to manage conflict because middle managers are often central to the organization's communication networks. Skills in listening, conflict management, negotiating and motivating are important for these activities. On the one hand, Ann only believed Joe, the current manager of the market research group whose suggestions to increase the market analysts salary if she want to increase their speed to finish every marketing research project and reducing the market analysts turnover numbers. She had not enquire other different marketing research managers idea why they can not finish every marketing research project quickly. What the problems are that who are encountered to cause to finish every marketing research project slowly. On the other hand, Ann could not know what the urgent jobs are who ought need to solve. When Joe, the current manager of the market research group told her that the company's intranet has been broken to cause a delay in the completion of an important market analysis. After she had not attempted to find the computer technical staffs to help her to repair intranet during the day and she still to read any email from her office computer during the overtime of the whole day. It proved that her time management is not effective to deal what the jobs are urgent and what the jobs are not urgent to do during the day.

If no, how well do you think she will perform better in her new job as head of marketing , if she can work in one time pressure reducing working environment?

I think Ann needed to attempt to find computer technical staffs to help her to repair intranet immediately and she ought not spend much time to see email, she ought continue enquire whether intranet had been repaired and the completion of an important market analysis had been sent during the day and she ought not spend much time to discuss to increase salaries matter to market analysts with Joe during the day. Thus, Ann did not know what the duties are needed to handle urgently during the day effectively. The most important, Ann needs to know what kind of job duties who needs to do as she is director of marketing clearly. This marketing research department is an internal department , every project team leader needs to manage and arrange every team member to finish every marketing research project efficiently and effectively. Hence, Ann's main duty ought to assist her every marketing research team to finish every marketing analysis before the due date to avoid to extend time to finish every important marketing analysis in this marketing department. Ann needs to know individual factors, e.g. learning ability, personality, values, motivation and stress and interpersonal factors, e.g. leadership, communication, decision making skill, intra and inter group
dynamic communications will influence her performance in her new job as director of marketing successfully.

I think Ann Wood ought to perform as these methods in her new job as head of marketing. However, She could attempt to produce a fair job description, it's an internal part of job evaluation process, grading and salary description, training is focused on elements of a job and how employees can perform better in their job. Aim to produce a reasonable salary to compare market salary level in every specific positions. Job analysis is establishing and defining every position correctly is from the starting point. Enquiring employees to complete questionnaires, observing and interviewing people. It aims to enlarge job enrichment, it extends the work of existing employees to cover more responsibility and decision making. Motivation is the act of getting someone to act on a situation in a workplace. Maslow's hierarchy of needs includes these level: The first level is physiological needs are basic needs to be met in order to survive, including food, water, clothing, sleep and shelter. The next level is security, staffs' surroundings are not threatening to them or family. If the environment seems to be safe, then it means stability in the workplace. Security could also include financial security. This could be achieved by creating a retirement package, securing job position and insurance. The third level is affiliation which is the need to feel a since of belonging or to be loved. In the workplace, this means to feel as though they are a part of the group and included in the work. The fourth level is explained as esteem. This is the view that one has of themselves, the person must have a high image of them self and encompass self respect. Feelings of self worth and the need for respect from others. The last and final stages of the hierarchy of needs is self actualization . This level is defined as someone being all they can be and they have met each of the previous stages. The person's talents are being completely utilized. The growth needs or the highest level of needs are the only real motivators of employees. Employees feel dissatisfied, so who unmotivated. For an employee to be true motivated, the employee's job has to be fully enriched where the employee has the opportunity for achievement and recognition, stimulation, responsibility and advancement.

Ann Wood can apply Maslow's hierarchy of needs motivation theory to satisfy whose staffs personal needs. She needs to make her staffs to understand that Ann (their head of marketing) feels they are important to this company by financial and non financial types of motivation in workplace compensation to them. Ann Wood (head of marketing) can attempt to implement these types of motivation into her specific new workplace. Her workplaces are suffering with employees who are unmotivated and overall work performance is failing. Currently her employees do not have organizational commitment, then there is no incentive to excel at their own personal goals and organizational goals. If these employees can discuss techniques are implemented in the specific work sites and she needs to make employees have not feel as though who have reached in the end of their career job satisfaction. Thus, her employees feel dissatisfactory to their jobs and they feel financial and non financial rewards are not fair to compare other employers in this market salary level to cause they intend to quit their current employer. She can use quantitative performance measurement to measure her employee work performance, such as absenteeism, project production turnover, extra hours worked as well as qualitative measurement, such as supervisor/manager ratings on appropriate performance . She can predict her staffs who feel dissatisfactory to their jobs from these information in order to enquire their needs. Often, the measurement will be used in part depend on what work outcomes are regarded as beneficial by her organization. For example, she can use rating form to evaluate every project team members of every one whose job performance from their marketing manager after every project team has finished its project. In conclusion, I give these suggestions to change her performance to deal her new job as head of marketing. For example: Removing some job controls, increasing worker accountability for them own work, giving workers free choice which projects who have interest to finish early, giving greater job freedom or additional authority to every project team members, making periodic reports directly to every project teams (not through every project team leader), introducing new and more difficult projects to give to the more potential project team members and assigning specialized projects to more potential project team members to attempt to finish, so who can become experts.

Assume Ann Wood wants her managers and associate to be the foundation for her department's competitive advantages. Use framework summarized to assess the degree to which Ann's people are a source of competitive advantage at the point of time. Competitive advantage means four key attributes: values, rarity, a lack of substitutes, difficult to imitate. Human resources are seen to be valuable, the cost of replacing employees who leave organization is high, who are experienced and are seen by clients as important. It results when an organization can perform some aspect of its work better than competitors or when it can perform the work in a way that competitors can't duplicate. The resource based view of organization theory refers the nature of human resource can be regarded as uniquely valuable to organization because who are a collection of asset (skills, competencies and experience) and are much more difficult to replicate, unlike other conventional asset, such as land or capital. Rarity is value or be a labour group which is short supply. Organizations have as stable supply of skills in short supply will have a competitive advantage. It is difficult to imitate skilled work of employees, change of services can be available. In instant, self service in restaurant but the market for high quality service by skilled employees are constant growth (Stredwick . J, 2005).

Human capital rareness means the extent to which the skills and talents of an organization's people are unique in the industry as well as human capital imitability means the extent to which the skills and talents of an organization's people can be copied by other organizations. Thus, Ann needs to employ staffs who are valuable, rare and difficult to imitate. If Ann want to lead her marketing research department efficiently. She needs to ensure every team leader has leadership ability and their marketing research skills and talents are unique in this marketing research industry as well as every team member marketing research skills and talents can not be copied by other competitors.

Thus, aims to assess the degree to which Ann's people are a source of competitive advantage at the point of time, who can follow these steps: Firstly, Ann Wood, head of marketing, who can attempt arrange training program is both quantitatively and qualitatively. Such training provides the base for effective of discretion by every marketing research team member. Reward systems that value in individual and team every project productivity help to encourage the type of behaviour that is desired. Giving responsibility and accountability complement the system. It aims to make every marketing research team member who can believe project should be fulfilling before due date, workplace should be fearless and energized, work and family life should be balanced and every project team leader should serve followers, every project team members should be treated like customers and who should not be afraid to make mistakes. This training program aims to achieve further lower turnover, higher satisfaction and stronger motivation among every project team members.

I feel the degree to which Ann's people are a source of competitive advantage at the point of time is not high. The reasons include as below: For example, Ann's one of staff Joe Jackson, the current manager of the market research group, who complained to Ann about the company's intranet had been down about half of the night and this technical problem had prevented timely access to data from a central server, resulting in a delay in the completion of an important market analysis on her first work day. He could not attempt to find any department staffs to help him to solve this problem. He did not know that whose some marketing research projects should delay if who waited Ann arrived office and then enquired her how to solve. Moreover, every marketing team members who ought lack enough marketing research working skills because who have no anyone could have confidence to finish every important and urgent marketing research projects before due date. Otherwise, if they had specialised marketing research skill, they ought spend little time to finish these urgent and important projects. So, the computer technical problem would not influence their projects to be finish. Hence, I think Ann needs to give them training to raise their marketing research skill if she still hope they can have high degree of competitive abilities to finish every further marketing research projects before due date.

Reference

Stredwick. J, (2005). An Introduction to human resource management. Elsevier Ltd, UK.

● Training and learning development raise baseball team members cooperative skill case

What happened with the A team when its baseball players feel to cooperate difficulty when the baseball organization lacks training and learning development?

One basketball A-team workload was sufficiently heavy to make task interdependence necessary and their performance outcomes (i.e. grades) were important to individual's academic standing (i.e. they were probation consequences for low team grades) and job prospects (for both recruitment and tuition reimbursement). Thus, when there were student teams, the work were a reasonable simulation of business teams with both task related work as well as social relationship and reputation consequences if the groups failed.

The fact that the A-team was newly forming and began their work with the same baseline resources was also important to this study in terms of differentiating the effectiveness of team conflict management strategies. Although A-team who have different expertise, but they have conflict due to different educational background and working experiences to cause A-team members cooperation will be more difficultly.

● Can lack training and learning training environment causes the baseball team players group feel cooperation difficulty?

This group process broke down because every member have different educational background and working experiences in their expertise field. They did not discuss who could do this team leader clearly For example, Aran suggested he could attempt to do this A-team leader because he was a management consultant in one large firm and his age was 52 year older than other four members, but the four members who could not agree his suggestion because they also had their expertise educational background and working experience. It should cause diversity conflict between of them. So, this group could not continue to discuss successfully.

What dimensions of diversity were responsible for the conflict?

Diversity is often defined in terms of particular dimensions, most commonly gender, race, and ethnicity, Other important dimensions also exist. These include age, social class, sexual orientation, personality, functional experience (e.g., finance, marketing, accounting), and geographical background. Visible attributable (e.g. race, gender, ethnicity), attributes directly related to job performance (e.g. education and functional experience), and rare attributes are the most likely to be seen as important. Workplace diversity could be a valuable asset for a organizational growth and development, e.g. age discrimination, not equal employment opportunity. Everyone has an equal chance at employment regardless of race, sex, religion, national original.

● providing training and learning training environment to baseball players benefits

In this university MBA A-team students team, the dimensions of diversity were responsible for the conflict were as the different groups of these five students should be treated equally that rewards should be based on merit (university project result) and decision maker (team leader) should be blind to the sex or ethnicity of MBA students to arrange their different roles and job duties to carry on doing this business plan project in their university. Hence, workplace diversity management can apply to this university MBA students diversity management. Workplace equal employment opportunity is similar to this university MBA A-team five students equal roles and duties opportunity as well as workplace organization decision maker is similar to this university .MBA A-team students team leader who needs to decide either employees or MBA A-team student team

members to pay attention to characteristics like sex or ethnicity to determine if who affect employment consequences or to arrange university MBA A-team five student members every role and duty to finish this business plan project. In workplace, every employer needs special actions , such as hiring the ethnic minority candidate when applicants appear to have equal qualifications, are considered appropriate requirements to remedy the effects of past discrimination and thus attain equal opportunity.

Thus, this university ought feel that it was such one employer, it needed to help A-team to choose one MBA student for A-team leader from whose prior working experiences and qualification. Then, it needed to give reasons to these other four A-team student members to explain why it felt this

MBA student was the best right applicant for their A-team leader. University professor Bowell group advisor might give probation period to this student leader if this A-team four members complaint this team leader who could not serve in the executive function to assign and oversee everyone's work and gave the presentation at end of project. Then , professor Bowell this team advisor might suggest them to select another new leader, so this A-team would not be disbanded easily. As this university selects the right applicant for every position. It needs committee to assist its selection processing. If the dean determines that the committee lacks diversity , it can be reconstituted by including persons from other departments or even other universities. The search committee chair must review information from candidates to ensure that minority and female and male applicants are in the pool. The dean's office reviews applications of diverse candidates of none of them appears among the search committee's choices of candidates to be interviewed, the committee must provide an explanation. Finally, the university team advisor ought be similar to an employer who needs to choose who are the top student candidates (employees) to make A-team (job offer) from their educational background, working experiences. It aims to reduce dimensions of diversity were responsible for the conflict.

● Describe which barriers to effectively managing diversity were present in this situation when the baseball players feel often need to be trained in learning and training environment?

Diversity can be defined as a characteristic of a group of people where differences exist on one or more relevant dimensions such as gender. First, faults can be present in situations characterized by diversity. Faults occur when two or more dimensions of diversity are correlated. For example, if all /most of the young people on a cross-functional task force represent marketing when all/most of the older individuals represent product engineering, then a fault is said exist. Faults merge multiple identifies (e.g. young and marketing focused) to produce barriers to effective collaborations within a group. Research on this phenomenon is relatively new, but has produced findings suggestion poor group outcomes. It can be applied to this A-team university team members conflict what barriers are to effectively managing diversity were present in this situation.

The barriers to effectively managing diversity were present in this situation , it is possible that this A-team group members who have different educational and working backgrounds to cause barriers to effectively managing diversity in this situation. For example, Rebecca is a young marketing manager for a large and high end Italian fashion company. She hopes this university MBA course can help her to be promoted to an executive position as well as Aran is 52 year old founder and CEO of an management consultant firm. He hopes this university MBA course can help him to retire from his consulting firm earlier and become an in house information system consultant to a large multinational firm. When she knew Aran promoted him to be this A-team leader because he had the most experience and he should serve in the executive function. Thus, he would assign and oversee every member's work and he would also give the presentation at the end of this project. Although, Aran have more confident to give reasons why he is the best person choice to be this team leader to manage every member and he also give useful suggestion that Cameron, an internet entrepreneur who heads his own small but successful company who will be in charge of analysing the financial feasibility of their project, developing the marketing plan, and evaluating the technical operations and the other members need to assist him. However, Aran is one managing consultant and Rebecca is one young marketing manager. Aran's educational and working experience is related to information system, but Rebecca educational and working experience is related to marketing field. Thus they have different expertise and skill. Rebecca feels that she has marketing field experience and she is younger than Aran. So, she have more ability than Aran to attempt to do a team leader to manage this A-team members how to produce marketing plan and report and presentation effectively. In conclusion, because these five students have different educational and working experience in their expertise field, so they feel themselves has ability to attempt to be team leader or attempt to do their job duties who prefer to choose by themselves. It will cause difficulty to any one team leader to manage diversity in this A-team members effectively and successfully.

CHAPTER THREE

Fair reward compensation strategy

● What is reward management strategy?

Why does organizations need reward management strategy that is concerned with the formulation and implementation of strategies and policies that aim to reward people fairly, equitably and consistently in accordance with their value to the organization. Reward management consists of analyzing and controlling employee remuneration, compensation and all of the other benefits for the employees. Reward management aims to create and efficiently operate a reward structure for an organization. Reward structure usually consists of pay policy and practices, salary and payroll administration, total reward, minimum wage, executive pay and team reward.

Reward is the generic term for the totality of financial and non-financial compensation or total remuneration paid to an employee in return for work or service rendered at work. Reward, which is sometimes been refer to as compensation or remuneration, is perhaps the most important contract term in every paid-employment. Its impact on workers (or employee's) performance is in most instance greatly misinterpreted. The understanding of this term is very important; this is because the incentive scheme given to an employee will influence the behavior and level of engagement to the organization. However, basic pay, it is a straightforward payment scheme which may not provide incentives to individual workers because they are not based on output or performance. This pay is often in relation to a given period like an hourly rate, weekly wage or annual salary. It's also an established rate for all workers in one category. Incentive for group, Plant/enterprise-based it is refer to as grain sharing within large group or the whole organization. This pay scheme is use in organizations where the workforce can clearly see the results of their efforts.

Award can include two kinds. Intrinsic reward include- Achievement, feeling of accomplishment, recognition, job satisfaction, personal growth and status, job enlargement, job enrichment, team working, empowerment. Otherwise, extrinsic rewards also include formal-recognition; base wage or salary, incentive payments, fringe benefits, promotion, social relationship and work environment. This study will explain and define different type of pay and non-financial scheme use in today's organizations.

Reward Management is concerned with the formulation and implementation of strategies and policies that aim to reward people fairly, equitably and consistently in accordance with their value to the organization. Reward management forms the organization relationship. This if an HR manager is to succeed in successfully managing the employment relationship, he/she will have to do well in reward management, otherwise these will be an in balance in the employment relationship, such as strikes, lockouts. Objectives of Reward Management may include: Support the organization's strategy, recruit & retain, motivate employees, internal & external equity, strengthen psychological contract, financially sustainable, comply with legislation and efficiently administered.

Basic Types of Reward include
● Extrinsic rewards
– satisfy basic needs: survival, security
– Pay, conditions, treatment
● Intrinsic rewards
– satisfy higher needs: esteem, development
Rewards by Individual, Team, Organization
● Individual: base pay, incentives, benefits
– rewards attendance, performance, competence
● Team
– team bonus, rewards group cooperation
● Organization
– profit-sharing, shares, gain-sharing

In general , a profitable reward management system should have these characteristics: Simplicity must be easily understood by everyone in the organization. People must understand why they are getting, what they are getting from the employment relationship . Fairness and equitability, every component of the system must be justifiable and consistently applied. But reward management has related problems, such as strike, staff turnover, dissatisfaction etc. An effective participatory reward management system should be negotiated and agreed better management and employees.

What is the role of Compensation and Reward in Organization? Compensation and Reward system plays vital role in a business organization. Since, among four Ms, i.e. Men, Material, Machine and Money, Men has been most important factor, it is impossible to imagine a business process without Men. Land, Labor, Capital and Organization are four major factors of production.

Every factor contributes to the process of production/business. It expects return from the business process such as rent is the return expected by the Landlord. Similarly Capitalist expects interest and organizers i.e. Entrepreneur expects profits. The labor expects wages from the process. It is evident that other factors are in-human factors and as such labor plays vital role in bringing about the process of production/business in motion. The other factors being human, has expectations, emotions, ambitions and egos. Labor therefore expects to have fair share in the business/production process.

What are the advantages of Fair Compensation System? Therefore a fair compensation system is a must for every business organization. The fair compensation system will help in the following:

● If an ideal compensation system is designed, it will have positive impact on the efficiency and results produced by workmen.

● Such system will encourage the normal worker to perform better and achieve the standards fixed.

● This system will encourage the process of job evaluation. It will also help in setting up an ideal job evaluation, which will have transparency, and the standards fixing would be more realistic and achievable.

● Such a system would be well defined and uniform. It will be apply to all the levels of the organization as a general system.

● The system would be simple and flexible so that every worker/recipient would be able to compute his own compensation receivable.

● Such system would be easy to implement, so that it would not penalize the workers for the reasons beyond their control and would not result in exploitation of workers.

● It will raise the morale, efficiency and cooperation among the workers. It, being just and fair would provide satisfaction to the workers.

● Such system would help management in complying with the various labor acts.

● Such system would also bring about amicable settlement of disputes between the workmen union and management.

● The system would embody itself the principle of equal work equal wages. Encouragement for those who perform better and opportunities for those who wish to excel.

Factors affect an organization's reward policy and strategy which include: affordability, it means what an organization can afford to pay the argument is that an organization can't borrow to reward employees, but should reward from the value created by the employees themselves. However, an organization has to afford to pay above legal minimums, legislation sets the minimum base pay (minimum fixed pay rates), which becomes the starting point in calculating for all of an organization's policies. Workers committees/trade unions depend on the power of a union, pay levels are determined through collective bargaining. The most powerful ones will strike higher levels, external job value means the market value of the job, e.g. what is the market value or HR manager or clerical assistant? Internal job value means the value or perceived value of a job compared to other jobs which the organization will determine the reward that job, e.g. HR manager compared to finance manager. Value of the person means employees holding similar jobs can be paid differently depending on the value of the organization performance and the economy environment influence means (labor supply/demand). Some authors explained a depressed economy increased the supply of labor, which reduced its price and have effect reward policy strategy.

Thus, reward system strategy means a benefit plan management procedure and it needs to implement these steps in order to achieve its fair reward as below:

Step one, deciding objective to assess what the company wants to achieve through its benefit strategy and policy, and its ability to pay for the changes;

Step two, obtaining view points and input from employees to collect employees' view points through employee surveys, focus groups and individual interviews;

Step third, analyzing competitiveness to establish or determine the company's competitive position, though conducting a customized survey or collecting available market data from external providers;

Step fourth, designing the benefit package to determine the mix and scale of the benefit package, the allocation of benefit, the scope for flexibility and the cost of benefit provision;

Step fifth, consulting the senior management team and employees on the proposal to get input and buy in from senior management team to make amendments if necessary, collecting comments and effort the non-financial rewards as benefits; step sixth, planning the communication to inform everyone concerned what is happening, why it is happening and how it affects them,

The final step , evaluation to review the plan on a regular basis and obtain input from employees and management for evaluation purposes.

Strategy reward system pay for perform two elements: Financial reward includes base salary, pay incentives, employee benefits. Non-financial reward includes intrinsic rewards, centers in the work itself, praise, recognition , time off. Reward system is a key driver of-HR strategy, business strategy organization culture strategic reward system related to HR system. Such as skill-based pay to training, overtime pay rules to labor relations, sign-on bonus to employment, merit pay to performance management and merit pay to performance culture.

Thus one successful reward strategy system will have these characteristics. Performance and reward strategy, identify requirement and develop strategy, analyze data and performance and reward information on individuals or group and achieve colleges to aid decision making, work with managers to certain and develop reward requirements for key individuals within their area, review and analyze the organization strategy demographic profile and market activity against current reward activity to identify current reward activity to identify current and long term reward requirement to assess internal and external factors driving reward requirements against plan. Explain to employees how pay and reward fits and supports overall people processes and activities, such as performance management.

In conclusion, what is award's aim ? For the organisation, reward should aim at; recruiting the quantity and quality required, encourage suitable staff to be loyal and remain in the organisation, provide rewards for good performance and incentives for further improvement in performance, maintain appropriate differentials relative to values of different levels of job, the reward adopted by organisation should be flexible enough to accommodate changes in the market rate for different skills and should be cost effective. For individual employees the reward system should be fair and equitable in valuation of the worth in comparison with others. The third which is the union of employees, the system should ensure maximum benefits for members without undue prejudices to their future security by making their reward to pace with the cost of living and the prosperity of the organisation.

What kinds of benefits of reward strategy which can bring to organizations? Good employee benefits and services can help the organization by reducing potential employee discontent, satisfying their needs and discouraging labor unrest or raising labor turnover. Thus, with competitive benefit programs , an organization can be more effective in recruitment and employee retention, thus reducing labor turnover.

Employee benefits may include legally required payments, such as workers compensation, long service pay or retirement payment, sickness allowance and end of year payment, bonus as well as optional welfare plans, such as life insurance, medical/hospital /dental coverage to self and family' education allowance, housing allowance, quarters, subsidized loans, retirement, pension plan, meal allowance, travelling allowance, paid time off, pay sick leave, other special paid leave, five day week, paid annual leave and maternity leave.

Employee service mean the organizations can choose to provide various services ranging from work related to those satisfying personal or family needs, in order to encourage employees to work happily and stay with a particular organization. The service may include social functions or recreational activities, e.g. New Year dinner, annual ball, company picnics, free transportation service, food service or canteen ,purchase of used equipment no longer required by the company, credit unions, low-interest loans, legal services, child care and elder care services, free holiday apartment, air ticket allowance etc. employees' welfares.

● Why does organization need reward management system?

Some HR professionals feel reward management can earn these benefits to organizations. In compensation and benefits reward management aspect, it is not possible to imagine an offer of employment that does not indicate a salary or wage and possibly other terms of compensation as well as description of the various benefits available with the employment. So, a candidate accepts or rejects the job offer, he/she will regard how a compensation package with a monetary of non-monetary value, such as a fair exchange for whose labor. So, the award management plan will include monetary reward and non-monetary reward both is better than monetary reward only. For example, piece rate pay is good for factory workers, commissions have long been a major part of the compensation of salespeople and merit pay and bonuses are well established methods of rewarding good performance for car salespeople. So, the variable or incentive pay is a good reward implementation plan for salespeople, insurance agents.

How to evaluate the base pay level is the more accurate? Leon, M. (2002) indicated that when a company needs to determine levels of base pay, the best companies have several objectives. The most important , in a global business environment characterized by strong demand for talented experienced employees is to be competitive. The determination of base pay level does not depend on only in one's own industry, but also in other industries competing for the same talent. In fact, a firm's closes competition for human resources often is not its closet industrial competitor. In addition, the best companies are attractive to the levels of compensation appropriate to the different regions and countries where facilities are located or where workers originate. At the same time, some are developing truly global talent managers, whose pay scales are most pay level to similar manager in other companies than they are with typical rate of pay in either the firm's headquarter country or its overseas locations.

Is one company achieves higher profits, it needs to raise higher wage to its all employees? I feel that it depends on whether situations to make decisions to raise all employees' wages , due to it has higher profit reason in the year. Robert, P.V. (2006) summarized these rules in dealing with subordinates, their performance should be enhanced. These rules includes using fair differential rewarding, it means that many managers try to treat all subordinates alike. When all employees receive equal rewards, superior performers begin to feel that their efforts are unappreciated, when poorer recognize that they won't be penalized for minimal effort. In response, over time, most above-average performers will drop their performance to the minimal level.

A few superior performers may persist absolutely , but most will lower their efforts to the level that they feel equals their rewards. So, when rewards are commensurate with performance, however, subordinates receive a quite different message. Superior performers get the signal that their efforts are valued, and potentially high performers are encouraged to try harder, identifying valued rewards for individual , it means that if a manager hopes to influence an employee's behavior through the use of rewards, the rewards must have value to the employee. One of the best ways to obtain such information is simply to ask employees what rewards they could like to receive. Younger workers may prefer more paid vacation days, (non-monetary value reward) or greater participation in decision making (high position management role) . The older workers may choose better medical insurance or a longer contribution to their pension plan, instructing subordinated on how rewards are tied to performance. It means that in order for maximizing organization's effectiveness, employees must clearly understand how rewards and performance are connected. When specific information is lacking, subordinates may try to second-guess their manager's intentions by constructing their own imagined system of rewards. Thus, much under productivity can be avoid of a manager clearly states goals for performance and explains how rewards will be related to performance, providing information feedback on performance means that in order to meet their manager's standards of performance, employees must have instructive feedback. Their manager must evaluate their information for them, indicating how well or how poorly they are doing and suggesting specific ways to improve. In addition to providing guidance, feedback can also serve as an additional form of suggestion.

Thus, when an organization earns higher profit, it seems that it ought not raise all employees salaries to be higher, because some hard working employees will feel unfair if the lazy employees can raise the same salary level to same to the hard working employees in the year. On the consequence, the hard working employees will be possible to under productivity or productivity in below level efficiency or inefficiency to perform their unsatisfactory or disagreed feeling to complain whose employers. Then, the organization will encounter low productivity in possible. Hence, fair reward management plan to all employees which is needed in any organization.

● Why do IT and bank and property management and school organizations need reward management system?

In IT and bank and property industries which need reward strategic reasons: Reward management systems have major impact on organization capability to catch, retain and motivate high potential employees and as a result getting the high level of performance. I also believe reward of employee performance can lead to differentiation between the productivity of the bank employees. In fact, bank employee performance is originally what on employee does or does not do. Performance of employees could include quantity of output, quality of output, timeliness of output, presence at work, cooperativeness.

Reward management in bank service industry, bank organization needs have effective and attractive reward management system to attract talent human resource applications. But banks are facing global saving bank competition. Reward management system is a core function of human resource discipline and is a strategic partner with company management. An good reward management can raise bank service employees performance in loan, saving mortgage etc. different departments. An effective reward management system can shorten service timeliness to raise talent employee individual bank service performance, raise the talent employee team cooperative effort in loan, mortgage, counter etc. different service departments.

However, reward management system tool includes both financial and non-financial rewards which are also called as extrinsic and intrinsic rewards. In bank industry financial rewards include salary increase, bonus, commission, housing loan allowance, education loan allowance. The non-financial rewards include promotion and title, authority and responsibility, appreciation and praise, participation to decisions, vacation time, comfort of working place, social authority, customer and management positive oral and written feedback, flexible working hours, design of work recognition , social rights, etc.

Property management industry reward management practitioners include property managers, caretakers, attendants, security guards, facility maintenance workers and cleaners. It is essential for employers to formulate strategic plans and coordinate labor relations of human resource with the development. In responds to the people-related challenge and opportunities to property management industry. It includes six aspects: communicating and improving staff benefits, promoting work-life balance and health and enhancing work arrangements, enhancing staff's career development and promotion prospect, improving the professional image of the industry, friendly employment practices for mature persons. Through these practices enterprises can make their job vacancies about attractive and answer misunderstandings about the property management industry.

Thus, the manpower shortage challenge will be avoid , when the people have interest to join the industry and they feel the reward is attractive to them to develop career. How to improve staff benefit? It includes new recruit entry bonus schemes, giving out little gifts and bonuses, during celebrations and festive occasions, and granting gratuities to critically ill employees or on the death of the employee's immediate family members, offers employees insurance plans, offering award schemes for employee's children by granting scholarships to outstanding students in recognition of their excellent exchange scholarships are available to subsidize their children's study abroad, promoting working-life balance to staff, such as organizing interest classes, setting up sports teams, organizing gatherings, participating in charitable activities, encouraging employees to organize social gatherings, promoting happiness at work, strengthening occupational safety and health arrangements to employees, e.g. setting up occupational safety and health committee / departments, formulating occupational safety and health policies, entertainment of work arrangement: compressed working days, five-day work week, flexible working days, flexible rostering, job sharing, part time work pattern, most rest time for frontline employee, job nature or workflow modification / re-engineering, improvement of employee's workplace environment, intra-district redeployment.

Reward is an important element in information technology industry. The IT industry had been needing a leader in changing traditional compensation strategy. Pay for performance needs to be designed effective reward system to encourage IT employee to work hardly in order to reward and contribute the most to an IT organization's technological productivity and profits.

The compensation mix depends on deliverable and the impact it has on the IT business. Consequently higher the responsibility greater the variable content in the pay package. IT industry has many IT professionals , such as programmers, software or hardware engineers, e-commerce website designer etc. different IT professionals. Hence, different IT professionals need have different skills to evaluate pay performance level fairly. However, performance related pay plans, it is a motivator the improves productivity. It helps in improving IT product productivity and performance levels when making every IT professional individual equally to encourage or motivate them to work to hardly in their IT unique professional aspects. It is a greater motivator for top performances and teams as they can get fair and reasonable reward and pay according to their contributions.

In fact, there is no standard formula for a performance -related incentive plan, it is unique for each IT professional. However, the incentive plan should need to be design to each IT professional with an organization's objectives. They include, communication and understanding of objectives, consideration of different IT professional performance against objectives, translating evaluation into the kid of IT professional performance rating, a link between ratings and pay to the kind of IT unique professional skill.

University HR strategic reward management system(review promote monitor scheme) aims to improve systems and skills for teaching employee communication, support teaching management to play a move active role in communication key messages, ensure school reward policies and procedures are fair to teaching staffs and administrative non-teaching staffs in salary rank increasing level, establish improved consultation procedures at academic and teaching service level, demonstrate the values and ethics by the university through management practices and communication with teaching staffs and non-teaching staffs, improve the profile and performance of the university by recruiting and developing talent teaching employees with appropriate external recognition , certain academic disciplines present more different recruitment challenges and profile of the university as an employer could be improved in the academic labour market, recruiting sample of selection decisions through early stages of employment to assess quality of appointment and identify learning points, support and encourage recruitment messages to improve selection practice including skills and high quality appointment decisions, raise the profile of the university as an employer regionally, nationally and internationally, establish succession planning for all key roles and positions linked with clear career progression with job families, to face in a difficult economic climate the university needs to continue to attract and keep high quality staff to work in an efficient and cost effective manner. The extension of workload allocation models to all academic units is an important tool to assist in managing workload fairly and more effectively, well targeted and designed training and development is very effective in motivating and enabling staff and support productivity.

● Why do small organizations need reward strategy?

Reward strategy can be applied to large organization, it can be also applied to small organization, e.g. family business, family business also needs compensation policies, the result encourages professional growth among family members and other employees as well as strategic business goal accomplishment. In general, compensation can be divided into the categories of base pay (equity as a basic for fairness , benefit, e.g. health care insurance, salary , wages, incentive compensation (e.g. bonuses, deferred compensation, stock or share options) and perks e.g. club membership, use of the company's private mountain, beach for holiday entertainment or sport activities e.g. free golf sport and company 's automobiles to provide to employees to drive in their private time.

Craig, E. A (2011) indicated that although small business has less employees , but it also needs compensation adjustments. The reasons include: (1) performance-based increases i.e. a rise, (2) annual wage adjustments e.g. cost of living increases to remain with what comparable businesses are paying and corrective adjustments to more pay for a position into with other position in the business increases are considered to be a key component of compensation by managers and non-management employers alike. The difference between one small organization's and one large organization's performance based increase is possible that one large organization has more a rise amount of performance -based increases in every time performance review. Otherwise, one small organization has less a rise amount of performance -based increases in every time performance review.

A good reward strategy can develop a philosophy of compensation that builds a framework for base pay and incentive tailored to the special values, goals, and needs of the particular family firm. Hence, one family or small firm's compensation -reward strategy can be explained to be needed, due to these factors : the firm can compare pay and performance levels with those of businesses with whom which compete for employees, the firm's goal is to provide total compensation between median and the percentage of comparable groups, base salary will be made more accurate decision at or high or below the median level for the comparable groups, individual salaries will be made more accurate decision within how much percent of the midpoint for the firm's comparison group's salary range, the firm can make more accurate decision on emphasizing whether performance -based incentives ought be spent at the expense of the salary, whether annual incentives ought be exceed those of comparably sized competitors, whether long-term incentives ought be based on results that add shareholder value.

However, culture can influence some business owners how to make compensation issues, culture means beliefs, values, assumption, habits and behavior patterns of the organization. The reasons staffs are paid the way, they are may be partly unconscious and may arise from the personal and family history and the deeply felt personal needs of the business leader or leaders. So, any family or small business will ought try to develop a philosophy of compensation (reward) strategy , which may learn a great deal about itself in the process. For example, a entrepreneur has confidence in her or his ability to manage compensation on a case-by-case basis and maintain tight personal tight personal control over each individual pay, perks, incentives, dividends, and gifts in order to encourage its employees can raise more effort to increase the sale number to its different kinds of product in its shop. Otherwise, if a family member working in this kind of culture asks for a raise, the business owner will not talk to about how to raise compensation to his/her salespeople in Christmas period. Hence , culture seems to influence the large organization and small organization how to make itself compensation to salespeople in Christmas period.

However, a basis for fairness to base pay which can let the large organization or small organization's staffs to feel, it is very important , when the large or small organization needs to focus on filling a vacancy and getting new skills into key areas quickly to meet customer needs with quality and efficiency. Because if the large organization or small organization expects it sale turnover may increase or staff turnover may decrease, but hiring needed talent may become more difficult, indicating that the company's pay structure may have lost internal logic if it's basic pay is unfair to attract talent staffs choose to join to its organization to work, when they feel that the organization's base pay is not reasonable to compare its competitors (pay for one job compared to another), and comparable jobs outside the company, the process is logical , objective and fair to be needed to judge the base pay structure to any organizations. Having a consistent, explainable ration for how compensation or reward is critical for employee and shareholders judgements about fairness. Hence, individual employee will usually compare his/her job in the company's salary and his/her similar job in another company's salary whether whose salary is same or more or less between whose company salary and similar company salary. Hence, a company needs to establish equitable base pay in a market value and merit system, with any adjustments , pay raises being a function of performance merit in order to make more reasonable compensation or reward to let its staffs to feel to avoid staff turnover number raises.

A rational compensation system steps can include: creating job description for all jobs, conducting a job evaluation to rank order jobs and determining which jobs that are similar in their importance to the business, obtaining external wage and salary survey information for representation jobs, utilizing other sources for comparable external data when needed, determining the company's reward strategy for compensation and deciding whether it wants pay to be set at the market average , whether it wants compensation at levels above or below the market average, or whether it wants to make a culture statement with pay levels, creating a wage and salary structure of starting pay levels, (minimums) and levels of pay for the most experienced workers (maximums). Analyzing current pay levels against the new structure pay levels against the new structure to determine which jobs are paid appropriately and which ones are not, considering individual, unique jobs that may have qualitative more or less important than external market comparable might suggest, making pay adjustments for those that are not of the range, accelerating regular increases for positions below the target range and decelerating or not making increased that are above the range. Finally , it needs to periodical check or review the wage and salary structure against outside bench market (external similar competitors positions to maintain external equity).

The point factor job evaluation tool can help the organization to make decision whether the staff ought pay how much salary level is the most reasonable. The point method include the elements such as : The experience element means the factor appraises the length of time normally required for an individual to acquire the necessary knowledge and ability to affectively perform the duties of the job. The experience level element means that whether the worker individual working experience in the firm, e.g. up to three months, he/she can earn the lowest points, till to comprehensive over right years, he/she can earn the highest points. The direction of others element means this factor appraises the responsibility to the job , it includes for organization, selection , assignment , guidance and review of personnel and the performance of other supervisory tasks. The direction of others level can indicate the employee earns none points when whose jobs involves no responsibility or authority for the direction of others, till to the highest points when the employee can confirm to own administrative ability,whose job is responsible for general administrative or executive supervision of all or broad segment of company operations as well as he/she can establish general policies and procedures and formulates and applies broad plans of operations.

Compensation specialists can help the company to select representative jobs from a company and find good external comparisons. They will need to make adjustment. Some criteria for determining a jobs' market value can include position title and job description, industry, size of company, sales or revenue volume, cost of living, based on location etc. data to determine whether their company's salary level is acceptable or reasonable to a job's market value. They need to gather the data concerns the job's market value. This is helpful because the latest supply and demand factors can affect certain positions may not show up in surveys. They must need to gather similar industry's organization size, sale or revenue volume data, daily cost of living and transportation cost how to influence their employees' income and similar competitors' employees income in order to make more reasonable and accurate salary structure adjustment.

● Reward management aims to bring positive influence to work performance, how to achieve high work performance?

How can reward management strategy raise job performance? In organization, work performing is affected by job characteristics and physical work environment, ability and skills and the willingness to performance to the individual employee. The major strategic rewards decisions to reward employees which include: What to pay employees, how to pay individual employees, cognition programs? Concerning about what to pay? The employer needs to establish a pay structure balance between internal equity, (the value of the job for the organization) and external equity , the external competitiveness of an organization's pay relative to pay in its industry.

What does reward management mean? The management discipline is concerned with the formulation and implementation of strategies and policies, the purpose of which are to reward employees fairly, equitably and consistently in accordance with their value to the organization. It deals with design, implementation and maintenance reward systems (processes, practices, procedures) that aim to meet the needs of both the organization and its stakeholder. Thus, total reward can include non-financial as well as financial element is developed, implemented and treated. Usually , the components of total reward include two aspects: tangible rewards (base pay, contingent pay and employee benefits) as well as relational intangible rewards (learning and development), the work experience and achievement, growth , non-financial rewards . Then, it is the total reward. However, reward can include these tangible and intangible elements: payment, such as salary, bonus, shares etc. Praise, such as positive feedback, commendation, staff-of -the year award etc. Promotion, such as status, career development. Punishment, such as disciplinary action, criticism, withholding pay. Thus, if one employee can not achieve the satisfactory performance, he/she ought need to get disciplinary action to be punished in order to let he/she learns how to revise his/her performance to raise working efficiency.

How to implement strategic reward management? Where do we want our reward practices to be in a few years time (vision)? How do we intend to get these (mean)? So, a declaration of intent that defines what the organization wants to do in the longer term to develop and implement reward policies, practices and processes, that will further the achievement of its business goals, and need the needs of the stakeholders, it can give a framework to other elements of rewards. So, the structure and content of a reward strategy may include: Environment analysis, macro-level, social, economical, demographic, industrial level, and micro-level competitors, analysis of job evaluation, financial conditions, gap analysis.

When the organization expected to apply reward strategy to raise employee individual performance successfully? It needs to know what job evaluation means. It is a systematic process for defining the relative worth/size of the jobs roles within a organization, for establishing internal relatives, for designing an equitable grade structure and grading jobs in the reward structure. For example, reward strategy can attempt to reduce wage gaps, when the wage gap can occur in the company, it can use international benchmarking in job evaluation. However, the cause is simple. The market of top managers is usually international, they earn international wage, or they leave the firm. The market of workers with little or no qualification is local in nearly every case. They can earn local wages. In less developed countries , this can lead to raise wage gaps between the top and bottom employee. Hence, if the firm discovered it has large distance of wage gaps between its top and bottom level positions. It ought need to find methods to adjust these positions' salaries to be reduce large distance of wage gaps fairly in order to let these large distance of wage gaps of position employees , they can feel their company is more fair to treat every employee.

Moreover, firm also need to consider that whether it ought choose which type of individual payment to excite its employee individual performance to be improved. They may include: performance -related increases basic pay or bonus -related to assessment of performance, contribution-related pay is related both to inputs and outputs, skilled-base pay is related to high or low skilled to the individual effort performance, service -related pay is related to whether the employee needs to spend how long service-time to satisfy customer's need in order to measure every service employee's performance, team-based pay is related to team performance, it can encourage teamwork, loyalty and cooperation and it can be demotivating on individual level.

All of these any types of reward method will improve or encourage the low performance employee individual working efficiency or raise productivity more easily as well as fair reward strategy can upgrade the high performance employee individual efficiency or encourage them to exceed their productive level or raise their productivity to achieve the maximum number. Hence, reward management has direct relatively to influence every employee's performance in order to bring either long term positive or negative influence to their organizations.

● What factors can influence organization's reward strategy?

What is reward management strategic principle to employment relationship? employees needs to pay tangibles (salary, wage, cars, educational , holiday allowance etc.) or/and intangible (recognition, career development growth etc.) rewards to employees aim. Individual balance to achieve tangible output, sales and/or intangibles loyalty , service performance, commitment. Hence, reward management forms the employment relationship, if an HR manager is to succeed in successfully managing the employment relationship, he/she will have to do well in reward management.

The reward management principle includes simplicity, it must be easily understood by everyone in the organization, fairness and equitability , every component of the system must be justifiable applied. This element is arguably the most challenging to implement and is the cause of most reward management related problems , such as strike, turnover, dissatisfaction etc. Hence, an attractive communication and training to the low skillful labour to have chance to upgrade high skillful which is needed, a participatory chance is effective one should ideally be negotiated and agreed between management and employees.

In fact, traditionally companies have always adopted the base pay strategy. It pays the legal minimum wages and salaries. However, it does not adequate in new work cultures and in terms of attracting , retaining and motivating top performers for strategic purposes, but still very commonly for lower level employees. The new reward strategic options include as below:

1. Knowledge and skills based strategy, because of the proven relation job performance, organizations have sought to encourage continuous skills development by trying it to rewards. A organization simply varies its pay structure according to one's level of knowledge and skill (job evaluation systems. It can define which skills, it values and will pay for and must have a

supportive training and development strategy. It is based pay with an equal base pay and a variation based on skills and knowledge. It may be costly in the short-term , but it is beneficial from a knowledge HR base through increased productivity and quality of product.

2. Performance based (varied pay based structure strategy), employees should be rewarded only for the value they create. A company will reward employee in the same grade variably depending on each employee's performance.

3. Incentive based pay structure strategy, it measures but being different in that it focuses on group performance rather than individual performance. The starting point in strategy is to define group performance targets , such as productivity sale volumes or profitability.

What factors can influence organization's reward strategy? They include: Affordability, the argument is that an organization can't borrow to reward employees, but it should reward from the value created by the employees themselves; legislation sets the minimum base pay minimum fixed pay rate; union/workers committees' pay level are determined through collecting bargaining. For example, strike issue will bring higher salary level in possible; external job value, the market value of the job, e.g. what is the market value of an HR manager or clerical assistant; internal job value, perceived value of job compared to the other jobs which the organization will determine the reward for the jobs , e.g. HR manage compared to finance manager; value of the person, employees holding similar jobs can be paid differently depending on the value to the organization performance; the economy changing factor (labor supply/demand) in labor market, e.g. it is a depressed economy increases the supply of labour, it will reduce the labour wage/salary market prices, due to the economy is bad , employers won't need to raise to any employees number and it has excess labour supply number to affect reward policy strategy.

    1.4 What is reward system of McDonald ?

For McDonald's Corporation U.S. employees at corporate, division and region offices, McDonald benefits are organized into four Performance management includes processes that effectively communicate , company aligned goals, evaluate employee performance and reward them fairly.

Your Pay and Rewards (ref from McDonald's reward system)

Attractive program follows a "pay for appearance" beliefs: The better your results, the greater your pay opportunities.

● Base Pay

Since employees' bottom pay is the most important portion of their recompense, McDonald's maintain the competitiveness of our base pay through an annual review of both external market data and interior peer data. In our business, division and region offices, McDonald's has a broad banding compensation system. Broad banding allows for suppleness in terms of pay, movement and growth.

● Incentive Pay

Inducement pay gives our workers with the possibility to earn spirited total compensation when performance meets and exceed goals. For our corporate, parting and region office, the Target Incentive Plan (TIP) links employee presentation with the presentation of the business they hold up. TIP pays a gratuity on top of employees' base salaries base on business presentation and their person appearance.

● Long Term Incentives

Long term incentives are granted to entitled workers to both prize and retain key employees who have shown continued presentation and can crash long-term value creation at McDonald's. for the befits of employees the long term incentives are very helpful because when the organization has a policies of incentives or long term incentives then the employees of the organization feel secured and work hardly for the organization. Similar like this any company or any Originations rewarding system always brought positive crash.

● Recognition Programs

Mc Donald's recognition programs are intended to reward and recognize physically powerful performers. For our corporate, separation and region offices, these take in the president Award (given to the top 1% of individual performers worldwide) and the Circle of fineness Award (given to top teams worldwide to be familiar with their aid for advancing our vision). Once start to hesitation your honesty, and then no one is leaving to alter their activities Appraisal system is also very helpful and makes a positive competition and encouragement in between the employees of the organization. Promotions will be appraisal based which encourage employees for hard work.

● Company Car Program

Mc Donald's company car program provides entitled employees with a company car for both business and individual / personal use. If entitled, employees can decide from. This is also very encouraging and motivating incentive for employees. It creates competition between employees and they work hard to get this incentive.

In conclusion, the assumptions the company is creation about their prospect service and its intention to support their progress. Practical processes for deploy people and delivering enlargement which are consistent with these intention. The reserve and promise for taking these types of program used. If we see in past we can get that simple ways in which the company could use the out test for the planed strategies and special and important clues for the good results.

Reference

Craig, E.A. & Stephen, L.M. & John, L.W. (2011) family business compensation: New York, US, Palgrave Macmillan, p.35

Leon, M. (2002). High performers, how the best companies find and keep them: US, Jossey - Bass, John Wiley & Sons, Inc, US pp.133-134

Robert P. V, (6 edition, 2006). organizational behavior: core concepts: US, Thomson, pp.58

● Electronic assemblies factory on performance increasing wage compensation strategy

Can this electronic assemblies factory implement on or unfair reward negative feeling influence electronic assemblies factory workers team real performance ? I feel that this factory workers' inefficiency does not mean they feel workload causes, it is due to they feel unfair reward , e.g. none on performance increasing reward method to cause their manufacturing efficiency to be poor in this electronic assembiles factory organization. I shall explains how and why one fair reward method can excite this organization manufacturing number to every workers. So, it is not due to shortage of workers number causes inefficient manufacturing, it is due to unfair reward to influence their inefficient performance more.

The best ways evaluate to measure what factors are seemed to be influencing this company electronic assemblies products manufactory factory workers team performance.

Firstly, we need to know what kind of methods which can be used to measure team performance, then, we can follow these measurement methods to judge what factors are seemed to be influencing this team performance more actually. Effectiveness and efficiency are the best ways to evaluate team performance. Efficiency is oriented towards successful input transformation into outputs. Effectiveness measures how outputs interact with the economic and social environment and it is being used to reflect overall performance of the team. This company electronic assemblies products manufactory factory team of workers could be evaluated team performance in terms of effectiveness. It's main focus is to achieve team's mission, goals and vision, such as whether how many workers could attempt to finish to wire eight assemblies an hour to meet their one client, Pacific electronic company to know how many assemblies of numbers had been finished to wire currently in order to meet whose Pacific electronic company client shipping schedule or not. At the same time, which value these electronic assembly workers whose performance in terms of their efficiency which relates to the optimal use of resources to achieve the desired output, such as whether how many worker numbers and machine tool numbers would be needed to provide to wire assembly numbers to finish in order to meet whose Pacific electronic company client shipping schedule or not. However, this team performance would have this question ,such as whether there was a difference if this team was effective yet inefficient. Hence, this team would face unprecedented

challenges (factors) which were seemed to be influencing team performance. The first factor was such as, it's client Pacific electronic company needed shorten time to finish wire assemblies which was the main factor to influence performance, such as this team workers would feel difficult to increase to wire eight assemblies an hour from three assemblies an hour, so who would feel anxiety to meet the shipping schedule to finish whose job and quality of assemblies production could not be satisfied to Pacific electronic company client possibly.

The second factor was such as, this company factory and office team management structural relationship. Usually, high team performance has strong upper management and human resource standards which had been set in place. Because of high team performance expectation, right staffs were being hired to fulfil the positions in order to employees were well aware of the performance measurement and the importance achieve the excellence in their duties.

Due to a high degree level of employee involvement needed to be in the team production process, the entity was awarded with staffs commitment which reduced rotation level and the cost associated with the hiring and training process. Hence, employees who were devoted to the team were well aware of necessary knowledge and skill and experience to create unique solutions for clients. Training can be an essential tool for maintaining and improving the productivity of staffs and relevance of skill. The ongoing shortages of labour and skill, the company should be taking action to reduce the impact of staffs scarcity by training staffs who already had employed.

Development opportunities were provided to motivate staffs by providing them with skill and knowledge enrichment . At the same time, a better skilled, more motivated workforce would help boost competitiveness, improved productivity and increased profit margin. Moreover, this company lacked good team communication relationship, such as Bill, factory team supervisor who only knew whose same workers of team, such as some of workers Dennis and Steve and Jack who would feel difficult because whose workers were supposed to wire three assemblies an hour normally with five years, but who were supposed to do eight assemblies an hour to sudden meet one client, Pacific electronic company client schedule to finish confidently as well as who would feel dissatisfactory, due to whose wages did not increase much more to pay for performance to the optimal compensation currently and these workers lacked enough training to face this sudden change to face this client's demand. Thus, it was possible that to influence whose team performance to be poor due to who could not adapt this sudden change from this client's demand. Due to Bill, electronic factory supervisor had not communicate to face to face to contact to enquire whose workers whether what reasons to cause who would feel difficulties if who needed to increase to finish wire assemblies and attempted to find solved methods due to sudden clients' demand. Hence, Bill could not have knowledge and skill to judge whether the reasons were either the numbers of workers or machines were not enough or both to cause that they would feel difficulties to increase their speed and effort to finish up to eight wire assemblies of numbers to meet this clients' current schedule sudden change demand at this moment.

The third factor was whether this company had effective strategic approaches to this team. A high team performance which maintains five major approaches: They include strategy, customers, leadership, processes and structure , values and beliefs. Strategic approach takes the team to a higher plan of maturity with a vision where the entity is going; customer approach strives for loyalty; leadership approach is associated with management knowledge to transfer the strategy
to employees (teams) level and which will have a direct impact on their behaviour and beliefs and teams' processes and structure and high performance team will strive for implementing innovative policies to

support team strategy; the last model is value and belief which translates into team ability to implement the strategy. In fact, this team lacked effective strategic approaches, such as Mr Martin, office manager did not told Bill, electronic factory team supervisor how to lead whose team to a higher plan to maturity with a vision where the entity was going, such as team lacked training or team lacked enough numbers of worker and machine to provide to increase to produce up to eight wire assemblies of numbers to meet this client's schedule shorten change demand to cause this team lacked evaluation to measure every worker individual effort to judge whether who ought have effort to already to finish more wire assemblies of numbers and who ought increase their wages due to they had more effort to raise more productivity to produce eight assemblies or more numbers. Hence, it caused the effort workers did not like to increase the productivity to meet this client sudden change easily due to who felt unfair treatment to compare the other less effort workers in this team. However, the Pacific electronic company client would lose confidence

to Mr Martin office manager if who could not accept Dave, shop of supervisor suggestion either to add some more incentive bonus to these workers to raise whose productivity or providing training or providing more machine and worker numbers to attempt to assist current workers ability to meet the client's schedule. Otherwise, it would cause this client did not choose to find its help next time again. The important factor was whether this factory supervisor and shop supervisor and office manager who had effective communication to predict how to solve any sudden clients' order change trouble between of them.

However, I think that, Bill factory supervisor lacked effective leadership to whose workers team in this factory, such as it seemed that some workers; Dennis, Steve and Jack who responded to Bill factory supervisor who felt difficulties to wire eight assemblies an hour suddenly. In fact, some of them had confidence to finish who told lie to Bill because Bill, factory supervisor could not be a good leader to know how to lead whose team to wire assemblies efficiently and effectively daily. Thus, Bill's leadership would have a direct impact on team workers behaviour and team performance poorly if Bill could not change whose leadership skill and who needed to facilitate workers team performance rather than to direct the team, due to who was a formal leader to their team. The company lacked value and belief with translated into team ability to implement the strategy, such as Mr Martin, office manager could not communicate with

Dave, shop of supervisor and Bill, factory of supervisor by face to face contact to discuss whether how who could raise to produce wire assemblies of numbers during any clients' sudden shorten schedule occurrence before, so it caused this factory workers team had not more confident to increase to produce more eight wire assemblies of numbers one hour due to this clients' schedule sudden shorten change. Otherwise, if who could often to discuss to suggest any methods to raise these factory team productivity, this factory leader, Bill would have enough time to plan already how to lead whose factory team workers to co-operate to raise productivity efficiency and effectively in this shorten schedule.

● suggestion time pressure reducing method

Identify the team norms and goals. Are they compatible with organizational objective when these factory workers feel time pressure is reduced?

What factors are seemed to influence team performance to cause these factory workers feel pressure to work in short time?

I felt that some of this electronic company factory team norms and goals are compatible with organizational objectives in some situations, but some of whose team norms and goals are not compatible with organizational objective in some situation. Norms mean rules or standards that regulate the team's behaviour and providing direction and are part of the team's mental model. When individual team members violate team norms, some type of punishment is usually applied. Although, norms allow teams be function smoothly, who can sometimes be harmful to team members. It is important that teams develop norms that both foster team productivity and performance and promote the welfare of individual members. This company goal was that it's factory team needed to finish identified wire assemblies of numbers to satisfy every business clients to meet whose identified schedules individually.

Hence, Bill, the electronic factory team supervisor who needed to follow Dave, shop of supervisor's instruction to inform whose workers team to finish all wire assemblies of numbers to meet every business client's identified schedule on or before due date. Thus, Bill , factory team supervisor needed to give team norms to let whose team of workers to know whose factory's rules or standards that regulated whose workers teams individually behaviour and providing direction to let them to know when (what the client schedule date was) and what the wire assemblies of numbers the team which must need to finish to deliver to whose clients by shipping.

Hence, this factory's rules and standards regulation could be one part to this factory team's mental models on this aspect to achieve this factory workers team norms were compatible with this organizational objective.

Although, the factory workers team norms allowed them to function smoothly, but Bill, factory supervisor could sometimes be harmful to the factory workers team to influence whether

the factory workers team productivity and performance standards level of those wire assemblies of products quality, such as Bill, factory supervisor informed to those factory workers team to increase to produce eight wire assemblies of numbers one hour for normal three wire assemblies of numbers one hour suddenly. It was caused these workers felt anxious whether who should be dismissed if who could not attempt to produce eight wire assemblies of numbers one hour from Bill, factory supervisor demand. It seemed that the factory workers team norms and goals were not compatible with this company

organizational objectives because this company organizational objective was needed workers finished to produce three wire assemblies of numbers to deliver to every client before schedule

due date. It was depended on the situation of the factory whether it had enough time and machine and skilful worker numbers to supply to finish the identified wire assemblies of numbers to every client identified schedule individually. Otherwise, currently, on this situation, it seemed that

this factory lacked enough worker and machine numbers and enough time and training to those old(current workers), it caused who felt difficult that every worker needed to finish to produce eight wire eight assemblies of numbers minimum per hour to meet this Pacific electronic company client's identified schedule change suddenly.

It also seemed that this company current organizational objective was not same to its prior (past)

organizational objective, such as every team worker needed to finish to produce three wire assemblies of numbers minimum per hour before to meet this Pacific electronic company client's

identified schedule change suddenly. It was given more difficult to let this factory team every worker to attempt to finish to produce eight wire assemblies of numbers minimum per hour

to meet this current Pacific electronic company client's sudden schedule change. Hence, in this situation, I should feel this factory team norms and goals were not compatible with their company's past organizational objective for this Pacific electronic company's earliest past three wire assemblies of numbers of every worker individual production demand in the identified schedule. In this situation, this Pacific electronic company client's wire assemblies of production numbers needed to be changed which caused this company factory team expectation schedule and wire assemblies of production numbers, such as every worker needed to produce eight wire assemblies minimum per hour of numbers of it's production goals and should be changed, but this factory team norms and production goals was still same to this Pacific electronic company client's earliest production numbers, such as every worker needed to produce three wire assemblies of numbers per hour. It meant that who needed have more time and worker and machine numbers to assist them to finish to produce if some workers had no enough effort to produce eight assemblies of numbers per hour to finish to meet this client's identified schedule change, otherwise, who needed to extend time to finish this client's production numbers schedule if none of them could produce eight wire assemblies of numbers at minimum one hour.

This, this factory team norms and goals
seemed that who were not compatible with organizational client's current objective to every worker needed to increase to produce eight wire assemblies of numbers per hour to finish to meet this Pacific electronic company client prior (not changed) schedule possible. Otherwise, these current factory workers could increase to finish eight wire assemblies of numbers to meet this client's current schedule goals. If this factory team some workers could finish eight or even more wire assemblies of numbers of numbers per hour individually. Thus, this team productivity could still achieve this client's expectation goals to finish to meet on or before schedule. It implied that this team norms and goals was compatible with organizational current objective due to client's expectation wire assemblies of overall increasing numbers had been finished to meet schedule from this factory team overall productivity together. Thus, it caused why this factory team norms and goals would be compatible with organizational team objective of finishing enough wire assemblies of overall numbers to meet this client's schedule date goals possibly or this factory team norms and goals would not be compatible with organization team objective of not finishing enough wire assemblies of overall numbers to meet this client's schedule date goals possibly.

● Does this organization lack fair reward on performance increasing wage compensation method to meet individual needs influence this team factory workers reduce manufacturing number?

This company, Steve and Jack were electronic wire assemblies products factory manufactory workers (members) among of this factory team, who had worked in this factory team five years. Bill was this company factory supervisor, who needed to supervise this workers team to help every business client to finish every electronic wire assemblies of products order to meet whose identified schedule, then delivered to them by shipping channel. Hence, if Bill, factory supervisor who could not lead whose workers team to co-operate to produce the identified electronic wire assemblies of products of numbers to finish to meet the individual business client's identified schedule before due date to deliver to them by shipping. It would cause that this company and the and the client would feel this company Mr Martin, office manager and Dave, shop of supervisor could not achieve their service agreement to finish electronic wire assemblies identifies numbers to deliver to them before schedule due date. The result would cause this company lost this client, even this company would accept guilty from this client's complaint. Hence, Bill, factory supervisor needed to lead whose workers team to work efficiently to achieve whose job responsibility to finish every individual business client identified good quality and non damaged of electronic wire assemblies of products of numbers to deliver to them by shipping before schedule due date.

In fact, this factory workers team was combined (co-operated) by every individual worker. Hence, if Bill, factory supervisor expected whose factory team could have good productivity and efficiency, who must individual needs. Otherwise, if some workers did not like to work hard, who would cause this team to delay to finish the identified electronic wire assemblies of numbers to deliver to the individual business client before the schedule due date. Hence, if ill, factory supervisor could satisfy every individual worker needs, then Bill could lead this team to perform more effectively and efficiently. If this factory work could be done by individual without any need for teamwork was not necessary in this factory. I supposed that this factory needed different workers worked in different steps to cooperate to finish every electronic wire assembly product. The reason was possible that because the employer felt every worker could be more proficient to practise to finish the identified step to co-operate to work together in one team, thus every worker could be raised productivity and efficiency in team, it could get more benefits than individual worker did all steps to finish every electronic wire assembly product alone in this factory. However, as the number of this factory team workers increased, the need for cooperation also increased.

As some point, the effort of Bill, factory supervisor who managed the factory team who would outweigh the benefit of having more workers and this factory team performance would began to decline. Hence, if this factory team of worker numbers increased suddenly. Although, every business client's electronic wire assemblies of products individual order finishing time would be reduced possibly, but it seemed that Bill, factory supervisor would feel more difficult to spend more time to lead this team to manage every individual worker who how to co-operate to work more efficiency and who should also feel difficult to satisfy individual worker needs if this team increased many worker numbers sudden seriously. Hence, this factory team overall performance of efficiency and effectiveness would begin to decline for long term due to this factory team increased many worker numbers suddenly to cause every individual worker felt that who could not satisfy more needs than before. Team structure means of coordinating formal team efforts. Leaders are appointed and work rules and procedures are detailed and job descriptions specify individual task responsibilities. It is necessary to coordinate the efforts of individuals assigned to the different tasks. Otherwise, tasks may not be performed in the correct sequence and employees may duplicate their efforts or work against each other. It seemed that this factory workers team which electronic wire assembling steps could be similar to bank loan department and collection department steps. If one individual worker who had much effort to finish whose wire assembling job step more quick to compare another less effort worker individual wire assembling job step. It seemed that the much effort worker could have much time to attempt to help the another less effort worker to finish whose step. Hence, it was possible that this factory team function could compare every individual worker's effort whether who could had more effort and time to help other worker to finish whose wire assembly job step during the less effort worker could not finish whose wire assembling step quickly.Thus, this factory team function could evaluate whether who individual worker had more effort and much time to attempt to help another less effort individual worker to finish their wire assembling job step for every individual client. It implied that these much effort individual workers who had needs to pay to optimal compensation more than the less effort individual workers for whose better performance in the factory team.

It was possible that the piece pay rate compensation was not suitable to these more effort individual worker to satisfy whose individual needs to accept in the team because who could increase return to multi tasking, in which the same workers did both easy to observe tasks, such as wire assembling production of every step and hard to observe tasks, such as process improvement of wire assembling production of every step and producing exact wire assembling quantities of output (no more and no less). I suggest this factory ought change piece rate compensation to time rate compensation and gain sharing payment method to the more effort individual worker productivity , the individual more effort worker who could receive time rate compensation plus a usually small amount bonus linked to the productivity of the establishment to this factory team during who could increase

return to multi tasking to assist whom to finish the another job step of less effort worker's wire assembling job duty for any individual client's wire assembling products delivering order before schedule due date. I supposed that this factory team function adopted transfer lines in which individual worker was

transferred between stations either by machines or by a moving conveyor assembly line. In either case, time rates compensation were more advantages than piece rates compensation due to

it was more fair to the every more effort individual worker if who could finish whose wire assembling individual step before schedule due date and who had more time to assist another

less effort worker to help who to finish whose wire assembly step immediately. In result, these every individual workers could raise this team efficiency to help this factory team to finish the identified wire assembly numbers to deliver to any client by shipping before the schedule due date normally.

Bill, factory supervisor and Dave shop of supervisor who both could obtain high effort from this factory workers on observable tasks by noticing where the wire assembly inventory piles up between stations, without incurring the costs of piece rates. I supposed that the wire assembling products required operations on different machines, performed in different orders setting up fixed paths for work to travel would have made low effort in production more observable, but would have made the wire assembling production process very inflexible. Therefore, Bill, factory supervisor needed put each individual worker in charge of a machine that could do several jobs. (each with a negotiated rat) and encouraged this team workers to do each job quickly via piece rates. Since there was recurring demand for each wire assembling product for a long time, management did not have to negotiate new piece rates very often. I suggested that Bill, factory supervisor should design the observable tasks , e.g. the step of wire assembling production to be done by one group of factory workers and the unobservable making improvement to the step of wire assembling production, fixing problems to be done by another group with a different compensation scheme and observable and unobservable tasks were separated in this factory team.

Thus, wire assembly production workers focused on producing output and were paid to piece rate. Quality was the responsibility of other departments workers, such as inspectors, who identified defective parts and engineers , who attempted to design less defect wire assembly products and processes, these all individual workers who every was paid time rates. All else equal, the low rates compensation was paid to less effort individual worker per piece and the higher rates and bonus compensation was paid to high effort individual worker per time rate to finish every individual business client's order. Finally, this factory team function could give synergy to achieve an effect of the total output of this factory team is greater than the combined outputs of individual worker working alone. In conclusion, this factory team function could use time rates and bonus compensation method to pay to the individual more effort every worker to let who to feel this employer was more fair to every individual worker performance. The more effort workers ought have more reasonable compensation to compare the less effort workers in this factory team.

● Can apply sale bonus on sale performance compensation method to excite Dave shop supervisor to raise sale number ?

If I was Dave, shop supervisor, what team concepts should I apply to achieve time pressure reducing aim to let these factory electronic workers to feel? why?

If I was Dave, shop supervisor, I should apply these team concepts to this electronic factory wire assembling team. When, managers assign associates to teams, who often make three common assumptions, which can lead to mistakes; such as, who assume that a large team size always better and who assume that everyone knows how or is suited to work in a

team and who assume that people who are similar to each other will work better together and so they can co-operate happily. Group means two or more interdependent individuals who influence one another through social interaction. Thus, if I was Dave, shop supervisor, I and my shop staffs would be one group. Bill,
factory supervisor and factory team workers who would be another group factory workers team ; Mr Martin, office manager and office staffs would be another group top managers team.

Our company needed these three groups communicate and co-operate to work together to deliver message between about of us about every individual business client's wire assembly product numbers demand and schedule due date to ensure when every client's order could confirm to finish to deliver to the client by shipping factory supervisor and whose workers was a team because this team had two or more workers with work roles that required them to be interdependent who operated within a large social system, as our factory performing tasks, such as every individual worker needed to produce every part of wire assembling in different stage relevant to our organization's mission , such as finishing the indicated wire assembling numbers to meet individual client's schedule to deliver to whom by shipping with consequences that affected others inside, such as Bill, factory supervisor and others outside, such as Dave, shop supervisor and Mr Martin , office manager of our organization, such as company and Bill, factory supervisor had membership that was identified to these on factory team and those not on the team, such as Dave, shop supervisor and sellers teams as well as Mr Martin, office manager and office administration teams. Effective team performance can be more difficult to achieve when team members belong to difficult identify groups or when their identification with these groups conflicts with the goals and objectives of the team, such as these factory some workers who felt difficult to raise to produce eight wire assembling from these wire assemblies in this factory team, but Mr Martin, office manager needed Dave, shop supervisor to notify to Bill, factory supervisor to let whose factory workers every one to know whether who could raise productivity to this eight numbers and who could not, then who decided whether how to solve that Pacific electronic company client could not receive wire assemblies of identified number before schedule due date by shipping.

In fact, Dan shop supervisor would had conflict, with Mr Martin, office manager who explained workers felt wages were less, so who would not worked hard to raise effort to produce more wire assemblies, but Mr Martin , office manager disagreed whose suggestion and who enforced Dan, factory supervisor to enquire whether these factory workers who could do eight wire assemblies possibly, it would cause some workers felt anxious to be dismiss if who could not finish this numbers. This, these group conflicts caused non effective team performance with the factory group goals and the shop group goals and management group goals which were more different. If I was Dave, shop supervisor of this electronic company, I would apply management team

concept to my shop group because I believed we were both the senior level shop manager and office manager who needed to coordinate the activities of our respective units, e.g. shop top management teams and office top management teams as well as Mr Martin, office management group . Otherwise, Bill, factory supervisor would be production team because workers who needed to supervise whose factory workers group to produce tangible products, such as identified wire assemblies

of numbers to meet every individual client's schedule due date.

A final consideration in Dave, shop supervising team effectiveness is whether a supervising team is needed to perform the work at all or whether the work is best performed by Dave,

shop supervisor individually.

In this case, it would have been better to have individual separately, Dave, shop supervising team effectiveness is measured on knowledge criteria, affective criteria and outcome criteria. Knowledge criteria reflected the degree to which Dave, shop supervisor individually increased its performance capability . Affective criteria addressed the question of whether Dave, shop supervisor individually had a fulfilling and satisfying to supervise shop experience, such as whether Dan could manage whose shop and factory effectively. Outcome criteria referred to Dan 's personal quality of the shop supervisor how to supervise whose shop and factory teams effectively. Hence, if I was Dan this electronic company shop supervisor, I shall apply these team concepts to apply to whose shop and factory teams management in this situation. So, on manufacuting number performance and on sale bonus performance compensation methods are suitable to shop supervisor and factory workers to raise their manufacturing efficiencies and sale performance in this electronic manufacturing and sale organization.

CHAPTER FOUR

Organizational Development Strategy

● Why do organizations need develop?

Organizational development (OD) is defined by theorists and practitioners in different ways. Essentially, it is a planned, organization-wide effort to increase an organization's effectiveness and/or to enable an organization to achieve its strategic goals. Before working on organizational development activities, an essential first step is to map the organizational context in which the changes , you are hoping what will occur. It means to understand function what affect your work, which approach you may be bringing to the activities and being able to determine an organization's readiness to work with you and develop for themselves the required innovations.

Many OD projects focus on providing the more visible material resources, building skills, improving organizational structures and systems. Moreover, culture values have an impact on several elements of as including: the way change occurs, perception about whether change is needed, perception about leadership and ownership , perception about risk and uncertainty, perception about relationship and partnership and perception of what success looks like. It is described internal changes as relating to organizational structures, processes and human resource requirement, whereas external changes involves government legislation, competitor movements and customer demand.

In general, organizational development aims to expect to raise awareness, e.g. improved understanding, attitude, confidence or motivation , enhanced knowledge and skills, e.g. increasing ability to act through teamwork, e.g. strengthened ability to act through improved with a group a people tied by a common task. This may involve for example, among them members, a stronger agreement or improved, communication, coordination, contribution by the team members to the common task, enhanced networks, e.g. improved processes for stronger incentives for participation in the network or increased traffic or communication among network members; increased implementation know -how , e.g. discovery and innovation with learning by doing formulation or implementation of policies, strategies, plans for UD aims in possible.

Why do organizations need to changed? Our business would is fasting to increase technology new methods of production and new taste of customers and new market trends as well as new strategies for best control of the organizations and motivation of employees like to accept to use new products in popular nowadays. Hence, managers need to concern how to decide about the change management in the organizations, because business activities now are globalize, and every organization needs to attract loyal customers , trained the employees, introduce and adapt new methods of production and best control the activities of the organization.

How will change organization in the good condition? The question arises in present scenario. Organizational change or change management aims to raise ability of the management benefits and support from change with reduced inefficiencies and ineffectiveness from the side of employees and encourage appreciate acceptance and support. The process of changing the activities of the organization as well as the implementation of the procedures and technologies to achieve the design objective. If the organization usually needs to change management includes different aspects, such as control change, adaptation change and effecting change.

Consequently, organizational change simply means to change the activities of the organization, it concerns change the culture of the organization, technology, business process, change of employees, rules and procedures, recruitment and selection, design of jobs, methods of appraisal , human resource , technology, physical environment of the organization, methods of training and development, job skill, and knowledge etc.

However, when the organization decides to implement change. Some employees should feel not adapt the change easily. They will quickly respond by complaints, engaging in work slowdown, threating to go on strike etc. How to overcome change management implementation successfully. The organizations need to implement change fairly , selection people who accept change, education and communication.

However, organization development also plays an important role in the change management. It can be defined as a collection planned change, built a humanistic values and benefits and welfare needs, that need to improve the organizational effectiveness and employees work performance and well-being.

● Why does General Motor organization need change management?

For General Motor (GM) change management case example, GM taking swift cost cutting action (2008) showed GM established in 1908s, till 1920s it was becoming the world largest motor manufacturing company, it could produce new style and design car every year. These were different brand cars which were producing by the company that time, and this every there were no other competitors to compete in the company different cars. But, the Japan automakers the company, GM felt threatened, specially Toyota Japan. Hence, GM needed to again get his position in market by restructuring and making change in the company. Now the GM company is again operating business in core brands in America, such as GMC.

GM taking swift cost cutting action (2008) also indicated that however, the change to GM was the high wages cost to employees as the company was paying US$74 per hour as compared to Toyota US$44 per hour, because GM was an agreement with trade union and GM run the plant with minimum 80% capacity whether it was needed or not.

Hence, what types of changes are decided to bring or make change to GM. In fact GM decided to bring changes on some areas of the motor business. These were included, structural change, cost change, process change and cultural change. The steps which as taken to change by the GM is about cost cutting, it has reduced cost of some brands to maintain the profit level. Similarly , GM also cut pay of employees which was the major problem. The GM also changed the culture of the company. GM removed it automate producing board and automate strategy up to 8 men board. It can changed the culture to improve the efficiency of the employees and such change is to speed up the day to day decision making.

But, GM also encounters problems to change process. Such as problems in cultural change, the cultural plan was based top down approach, which ignored totally the involvement of the employees as compared to other companies, some suggested that it has not down up approach in which employees feel satisfaction. So this regard , it empowered the employees by introducing in tailoring the down top approach. Rather then telling to employees what they do, due to its employees hope have change to discuss with top management to express their opinions. Moreover, the other problem with cost cutting from the agreement of trade union, as it was an agreement with not lowering the pay of the employees and maintain the capacity level.

Driving change at GM (2005) indicated that better result of cost cutting of GM seems from its employment figure of 98 to 2009. It was reduced from 226,000 to 101,000 workers and now the GM is concentrating on sale rather than to further cut off and also GM is deciding to reduce the worker force of the factory from 60,000 to 40,000. It certainly leads to cost saving to GM. Another better result of cultural change to GM, employees now becoming aware about the responsibility, as well as GM as empowered the employed to give better productivity. Hence, GM can success to solve change management problems to bring profit and win its competitors in motor sale market in global successfully.

● Culture can influence organization development

Culture is not the way we do things around here. Culture is which we cooperate and the through we view the organization. If we view an organization as a system of interacting and interrelated part, culture defines , creates and supports that system.

● IBM computer organizational culture influences whether it's computers will be out dated feeling to computer consumers

For IBM computer example, IBM had brought to change a culture means changing our fundamental view of how the world works. However, IBM ran into serious financial difficulties in the late 1980 and early 1990s in large part because it was unwilling to change the ways in which it was approaching the computer market, even though the market was rapidly changing around it to break with tradition.

How is culture created to IBM? Stephen, R.B(2011) indicated IBM founder , or the influential leader, had reinforced the values of culture. When he worked for IBM many years ago, he discovered the IBM leader was one considerable person to his employees. Such as one case, how when an IBM employee was badly injured and his family killed in a car accident, the leader Tom Watson was there at the hospital when the man woke up, promising to cover the medical bills and do whatever he could. Hence, he can let IBM employees feel that IBM was seem to their home family.

Hence, what makes a successful culture to IBM ? Stephen, R.B(2011) also showed that a culture is successful if it is in harmony with its environment and unsuccessful if it it unable to function in its environment. The environment is the world in which the culture operates. So, when environment changes faster than cultures. When the environment changes, the mechanisms of the culture may no longer be valid. Such as the advent of the PC changed the business environment for IBM, and the company found it difficult indeed to adjust. Today, with the accelerating shift from desktop computers to mobile devices and the Internet, Microsoft is still. In 1992, IBM had a loss for the first time, closed down numerous divisions. However, IBM's culture contained a very strong ethic of " analyze the problem, determine the solution, and execute the solution even, if it 's unpleasant." IBM realized that it needed a fresh perspective, so it brought in Lou Gerstner, the first non-IBM to become CEO. As Ed Schein points out, Gerstner came from a very similar marketing background to IBM's founder, Tom Watson, Sr. Gerstner didn't so much change IBM's culture as revitalize an aspect of it that had become dormant. Over the year, IBM's engineering culture had become dominant, and the marketing culture had benefit to become into the background.

● IKEA organizational culture influences whether it's China furniture market in success?

Why does IKEA management cultural diversity needs to regard its staffs in China challenge? Multinational company, such as IKEA furniture company aims to increase profitability and it also needs to seek to for solutions to problems related with the saturation of existing markets, it needs to make an effort to expand operations to overseas market, such as China. However, it will face cultural difference challenge to be needed to deal if it want to enter China furniture sale market successfully.

Kumar, S. (2005) indicated IKEA is the world's largest furniture retailer since the early 1990s. It offers a wide range of well- designed, functional home furniture products at low prices as many people as possible will be able to afford them. However, IKEA planned to enter China market, but it will face the cultural difference challenge between China and itself Swedish regional cultural of their staff communication and co-operational relationship.

In deed, the "IKEA" facilities its successfully international expansions , it needs to combination vision, characteristic leadership and business principle between China and Swedish culture effectively. IKEA opened its first store in China in 1998. Although, the company has succeeded with their global strategy in the past in most of the markets, it has entered , it quickly learnt the success in the Chinese market required a different strategy in the areas of marketing and HR (Kumar, 2005, p.2).

What are the cultural difference to influence IKEA's success to develop furniture sale in China market? The standardized strategy which is adopted by IKEA could lead to some disadvantages because Swedish managers are needed to send to other branches in other countries in other to ensure the IKEA way is implemented in the local areas. Thus, it brings the conflict between the Swedish management and local employees could occur due to the cultural differences. Especially, in the country like China where the traditional cultures and value are different to such as Swedish culture. So, Chinese employees will have their mind for long a working culture differs from the Swedish way that IKEA wants to influence to their employees, problems were unavailable.

When IKEA were keen to increase revenue in Asian markets like China, they faced the challenge to mange their staffs from the conflicts and the diversity of Chinese cultures, such as how to train people within IKEA perform in a standardized format to keep its essential value, and how to avoid the misunderstanding when improve employee performance and understanding the importance of cross cultural management between Sweden and China. So, IKEA managers definitely have responsibilities to spend time, energy and effort to understand the differences of national corporate and functional cultures before starting an arranging the strategic plans in China furniture sale market.

The another cultural difference challenge concerns China and Sweden both countries have problems on law, price competition, information, language, delivery, foreign currency, time differences and cultural differences etc. different aspects. Thus, such as this IKEA Sweden furniture international company plans to enter China furniture sale market. It will have great barriers are caused by cultural differences, such as difficulty of communication, higher potential transaction costs, different objectives and means of cooperation and operating methods.

These problems have led to the failure to IKEA furniture to enter China furniture sale market in possible. Therefore, IKEA needs to concern questions how to do business in China and understand China's culture and how to do business with Chinese people. It is possible that Chinese labors dissatisfy IKEA's provided cheap labor as well as the strong serious organizational bureaucracy system, high job duty demand is needed to satisfy customer's behavior in China. Hence, IKEA's culture difference challenge to China furniture sale market , it has relationship to human resource management and reward challenge.

● HR development organizational development aims

Human Resource Development is the framework for helping employees develops their personal and organizational skills, knowledge, and abilities. Organizations have many opportunities for human resources or employee development, both within and outside of the workplace. By the end of this paper i will be able to devise a human resource plan for a work area, to meet organizational objectives, identify and plan for individual development to meet organizational objectives and also initiate a personal development plan for an individual and evaluate progress. Healthy organizations believe in Human Resource Development and cover all of these bases.

The focus of all aspects of Human Resource Development is on developing the most superior workforce so that the organization and individual employees can accomplish their work goals in service to customers. We need to learn new skills and develop new abilities, to respond to these changes in our lives, our careers, and our organizations. We can deal with these constructively, using change for our competitive advantage and as opportunities for personal and organizational growth, or we can be overwhelmed by them. With all the downsizing, outsourcing and team building, responsibility and accountability are being downloaded to individuals. So everyone is now a manager. Everyone will need to acquire and/or increase their skills, knowledge and abilities to perform their jobs. By developing our knowledge and skills, our actions and standards, our motivation, incentives, attitudes and work environment we will be able to cope up with the ever changing work environment.

Reference

Driving change at general motor, 2005, online retrieved 15 Dec. 2009, www.cioleadershipnotes.com/p/gm/htm

General motor talking swift cost cutting action, 2008, online retrieved 15 Dec. 2009 from dailymarkets.com/stock/2008/11/24/General- motor-takingswift-cost-action-cutting

Kumar, S. (2005) "IKEA's globalization strategies and its foray in China", IBS center for management research

Stephen, R.B. Organizational development, U.S., The McGraw- Hill , 2011, pp.5-8

KBTZ television organizational development strategy case

● Can efficient development development strategy influence this television organization different departments' efficient cooperative relationship?

KBTZ was a large television station in United States. It was one of the largest revenue producers in its entertainment market and employed more than 180 staffs and it was as the local television leader in the use of sophisticated electronic equipment. The station's physical plant was planned to accommodate the new equipment and to boost its image at the leader in the entertainment market. However, its organization development caused much problems to need to solve. On the one hand, due to external pressure to cause organization change, such as entertainment market competition needed to have high technological new equipments to purchase to provide to different departments to use, e.g. cameras, films etc equipment. Hence, different department staffs needed to learn how to use these equipments to raise productive performance quality.

On the other hand, due to internal pressure to cause organizational change, such as reducing aspiration performance factor was caused poorly in KNTZ organization, which meant gaps was occurred between what an individual, unit or organization wanted to achieve and what it was actually achieving in KTZ organization. Due to KBTZ television station's operational department ,engineering department, programming department, sales department, news department etc departments which every department individual staff, work group, division or overall KBTZ organization was not meeting its own expectations to adopt KBTZ new organization changes as well as television programming needed new productive tactics to change new strategies and processes often caused follow poor performing individual staffs, units and KBTZ whole organization, which might reduce aspiration levels instead of making changes sufficient to increase performance. Because KBTZ large television station often compared itself with other television stations in the entertainment industry , when comparisons with similar others suggested that better performance was possible.

However, KBTZ staffs could not adopt organizational change development suddenly, so it caused many different departments felt difficult co-operation together in KBTZ television station organization. In fact, American television station entertainment industry was encountered by life cycle forces, it meant the natural and predictable pressures that built as to KBTZ television station organization grew and that KBTZ television station must hope to continue growing.

Hence, KBTZ television station was at elaboration stage, it meant KBTZ needed for balance, focused on efficiency and innovation, formal procedures existed and empowered low level

managers and associates in its organization if KBTZ still wanted to keep its large television station position in United States. However, KBTZ 's large television station's physical plant planned to accommodate the new advances equipment to provide different departments staffs to use and to boost its image as the leader in the United States entertainment market. It would cause its staffs feel difficult to adapt to adjust efficient and effective co-operation between departments due to it's planning change caused a process involving deliberate efforts to move KBTZ television station within its organization undesirable state to a new and more desirable state during KBTZ 's organization development was carrying on. Hence, due to its organization development change it would cause these basic problems at KBTZ organization as below:

● suggestion of organizational development strategy can reduce time pressure to any employees in this KBTZ television broadcast organization

As I was the KBTZ consultant to meet with Valerie Diaz, president and general manager, who explained the key problem as:

The first problem was the high stress to which KBTZ 's manager and associates who felt about time deadlines in television problem, e.g. when it's precisely six o'clock , KBTZ news department staffs must be on the air with the news. All of the news material, local reporting, news, interviews must be processed, edited and ready to go at six o'clock. This news department staffs felt difficult, due to who could not have any half prepared material extended deadlines to cause lose the KBTZ 's audiences. This situation caused a great deal of

conflict and turnover increased, such as a number of well qualified and motivated employees were leaving KBTZ television station. The news department's employee turnover was about 35% which was too high as well as KBTZ also had trouble hiring qualified people who fit their culture and these new qualified staffs feel difficult to co-operate with KBTZ staffs to cause conflict. It seemed to be team conflict problem.

The second problem was that business manager felt difficult to manage different departments, due to who previously worked in sales and in the general manager's office, but who lacked management training and this was whose first managerial position to help in managing whose departments.

It seemed to be personal difficult management problem.

The third problem seemed the news department and business office and programming department indicated who felt the new director who lacked leadership ability to manage any

departments, such as new department managers and associates felt extreme dissatisfaction with the department head, new director who had very negative attitudes toward their overall

work environment , new director lacked leadership ability to let news department managers and associates communicate easily. Moreover, news department associates also complained of very

low reward, including pay, promotion opportunities and managerial praise and who also complained of constant criticism, which was the only form of managerial feedback onperformance. Hence, it implied the new director did not attempt to solve any departments staffs difficulties to adopt new organization change to cause their dissatisfaction and conflict and complaints occurrence to whom. It seemed to be new director personal leadership problem and news departments staffs team communication and individual dissatisfaction problems.

The fourth problem was operations department manager who complained another departments, such as news department staffs, who were confused all of the time and engineering groups, staffs were lazy and who did like cooperation to influence operational department performed ineffectively, due to these groups needed to co-operate to work together. So operations manager suggested me (KBTZ 's consultant) dismissed chief engineer and shaped up (reorganized) the news groups and the engineers groups . It seemed to be difficult co-operation occurred between operations department and engineering and news both departments problem.

The fifth problem was chief engineers who complained the unreasonableness of certain people in other departments. For example, the difficulty indicated that whose team engineers could not immediately repair some malfunctioning equipment in their area and it could take several hours just to determine the cause of the failure. It seemed that engineer department

lacked enough engineers and equipments were provided to them to work from operational department . It caused team conflict problem.

The sixth problem was the program director complained the station was missing a lot of opportunities in other areas, e.g. news and sales, the chief engineer was incompetent and operations managers were difficult to motivate low level managers to make any decisions or took any responsibilities . It seemed the program director who felt dissatisfactory to other

departments personal performance problem.

The seventh problem was the promotion manger who expected a little training to provide in how to deal with people, innovation and communication problems. It seemed that promotion manager felt difficult to adopt new organization change problem.

The eighth problem was sales department representatives complained who ought to increase salaries due to whose good sale performance. It seemed that sales representatives'

dissatisfactory problem. Finally, the business office and programming department also made one survey to indicate

individuals in these departments to have generally positive attitude, such as job satisfaction, but who had two important negative attitude in whose working environment.In general, these low and middle level staffs whose negative attitude of task environment major problem indicated who thought that whose department heads and the general manager could handle downward communication better , it meant that the middle and low level staffs felt the top level managers lacked effective communication to them as well as these were several comments about being underpaid relative to other station employees.

Although, the survey indicated the managers and associates whose high satisfaction, but who also believed that the negative factors led them to be poorly motivated. Such as some low and middle level associates reported that who were not sure who was

top level immediate manager , since both the assignments editor and the assistant news director gave them assignments. It seemed that who lacked communication between departments to

influence who did not know who had actual authority to give job to them to do. It would cause difficult to co-operation to finish every job between department. If the assignments

needed to finish urgently, who would influence any news, entertainment programmes could not been finished before the time deadlines. It seemed to be team communication problem.

The another problem was that, some low and middle level associates also reported that creativity (thought to be important in the jobs) was discouraged by the director's highly authority management and structured styled as well as new director personal work attitude was not good style. It seemed that this new director had unsuitable personal management skill to lead this KBTZ different departments to follow whose guidelines to finish their jobs daily, to cause these departments ' staffs felt dissatisfactory to this new director's personal work attitude . It seemed that this was new director's personal management attitude problem. Moreover, this business office and programming department's survey also indicated these departments existed these problems in KBTZ television station organization.

Firstly, although most of operation department associates were satisfied with their jobs and reported pride in their departments and only some associates felt satisfactory about their operations department manager (head). All other some associates tended to feel overworked (reported a 74 hours workweek) and thought the department head expected too much and who also thought who were underpaid relative to their task demands and criticized managerial feedbacks on their performance and the department head never prised position performance and who only regarded them for poor performance and who also reported concern over the conflict with engineering group , but who believed operations and engineering department conflict, whose departments' leaders (managers) should be resolved. It seemed that this operations departments manager could not manage some departments staffs to work in normal hours to cause them to feel unhappy to work and they also felt underpayment and unreasonable feedback on the performance problem.

Anyway, the engineering department many associates were very dissatisfied with whose jobs and who had conflict to operational department and who also believed engineering department head did not support them and who lacked department meetings to receive feedback on their performance from the chief engineer. It seemed that this engineering department's chief engineer who performed more poor to compare to operations department manager to cause many associates felt dissatisfactory to him. Otherwise, the survey indicated that only promotion department associates had positive attitudes and their job satisfaction were high and everyone viewed their task environment positively and who had only few negative attitudes were primarily directed toward the ineffectiveness of the news department . It seemed that promotion department had none any problems, so its
associates could criticize the another news department ineffectiveness

result confidently.

Finally, the sales department's colleagues could not responded to the survey to indicate whether what kinds of problems who felt .Due to sale department head was the KBTZ

television station manager's son family relationship , so who could not respond to complete this survey whether whose feelings to this sales department manager was satisfactory or was not satisfactory to him, it would cause who lost their job if who responded whose actual feelings to me (consultant) to know at that day possibly.

● Which organization development techniques should I consider using and why?

As I was KBTZ television station consultant, I should apply these organization development techniques to solve this company problems. Organizational development techniques included relationship techniques, such as T-group training,

team building, survey as well as structural technique, such as management by objective and supplemental organizational processes. The news department problem, such as high stress to this department managers and associates. It was respect to time deadlines in television problem. The department's staffs must be on the air with the news. All of the news material , local reporting , news , interviews must be processed, edited and ready to go at six o'clock. So, this news department staffs often worried about extended deadlines or who only half prepared material or who lost the audience, it caused conflict and a

number of well qualified and motivated employees would leave this KBTZ television station organization and KBTZ also felt trouble hiring new qualified people could adapt KBTZ organization's culture to help KBTZ organization to raise competition in this USA entertainment market. On the other hand, due to news department staffs who were confused all of the time, so it also caused operations department manager who felt difficult co-operation with to cause operations department and news department would be often conflicts about news department extended time deadline issue.

Even, program department director also complained the station was missing a lot of opportunities in other areas, e.g. news and sales. I should use organization development technology, relationship technique T-group training to solve

this news and operation departments cooperation problem, which meant news department would implement group exercises in which individual focused on their action, how

others perceived their actions and how others generally reacted to them, so participants often learnt about unintended. Hence, this news department managers and associates who could

divided several groups, it aimed to focus on their individual action, e.g. local reporting group, news report group, interviews group, news material preparing group. So, these every group members (staffs) who could perceived whose individual group action and reacted to another group individual member action, such as news material preparing group individual member could focus on gathering news material preparing job duties, then who could gave news material to news report group individual member to prepare to analyse materials to prepare to report.

Another interviews group individual to prepare how much time needed and what places should be choose and who to be interviewed to prepare every day different news to let

audience to watch six o'clock news programs in television every day. Then, he could gave local reporting group individual member to analyze their every individual interviewing

record to produce every local reporting. Thus, T-group training benefit was that participants, such as KBTZ news department's material group individual member, local reporting group individual member, news production group individual member, interviewed group individual member who could often learnt about why unintended negative consequences were caused of

certain types of any group individual member's behaviour to cause to extend time deadlines or to cause only extend time deadlines or to cause only half prepared material due to very few time was enough to prepare precisely at six o' clock to ready to go before this news department all groups must be

processed to edit. Hence, group member which needed to finish whose identified group job, e.g. interview group members who only needed to focus on carry on training how to make date

and time appointment to meet individual in the beginning to till to how to prepare what kinds of interview questions would enquire and every interview was planned which needed how long time to finish. Hence, such as interview group individual member could review whose every interview progress to aim to achieve to shorten time to perform the better news programs quality to provide to television audients to watch at everyday six o'clock news time.

Hence, the news department's every group member could give chance to enquire survey feedback from every team leader (manager) to review their everyday news job to investigate whether whose group performance would cause unintended negative consequences to influence other group performance to be poor, such as investigating the day's news extended causing was due to the day interview group's individual member who could not organize overall interview procedure to arrange time to finish effectively or other group's individual member to cause. Hence, relationship technique T-group training method could review whether which group(s) to cause the day news extended deadlines or found whether which group(s) caused overall team which could not prepare all material to finish the day news

watching at six o'clock . It was one fair method to measure whether which group staffs were qualified people or whether which group staffs were not qualified people to co-operate in this news department.

Other problem was about business department head, business manager seemed that who lacked management training to prepare to do this position, such as who previously worked to do this position, such as who previously worked in sales and in the general manager's office only. Hence, who must need to provide training to prepare to know how to manage KBTZ 's television station organization different departments, such as news department, sales department, operations department, engineering department, program department, promotion department efficiently. As I was KBTZ 's consultant , I felt KBTZ could provide relationship technique of survey method

to assist whom. If every departments could get survey, then this business manager could obtain enough dates to meet all units to discuss problems easily. Then, when who collected all departments' problems from this survey, KBTZ could use structural technique of management by objectives method to assist him (business manager), it meant a management process in which individuals (different group members) negotiated whose group daily task objectives, such as engineer group

member could negotiate how much equipments who needed to repair urgently and how many equipments who could repair and gave reasons why who could not repair some equipments in

that day.

All departments might have task objectives to measure whose every group members performance to revise what factors caused whose performance to be poor in order to correct
to achieve every department's group member could raise work efficiently. Thus, this management process needed spend much time to revise every department's group individual negotiate task. For example, the business manager needed to meet engineering group leader (chief engineer) and members(engineers and technicians) to discuss whether how many equipments who needed to repair and whether how many equipments who needed to repair and whether how many equipments who felt who had no much time to repair this week, then next week, this business manager would enquire these engineers to revise whether what reasons occurred to cause who could not repair all machines last week. As this engineer department individual member technician who had negotiated task objectives to let whose chief engineer and engineering manager to know whether who felt that who could finish task to repair how many machines every week, then they could meet to attempt to explain what factors caused them could not repair all equipments further week. Hence, this business manager could used the same management by objectives structural technique method, such as every department individual member needed to negotiate task objective to finish every week, then who needed to meet whose department manager to revise what factors influenced their work efficiency, e.g. news department material group could meet to discuss task objective about how much time and how many staffs who needed to prepare to gather any related material to report this week ; interview group could meet to discuss task objective about how much time and
how many staffs who needed to prepare to organize any effective interview procedure to prepare individual interview this week ; news edited group could meet to discuss task objective about how much time and how many staffs who needed to be edit for daily news this week.

Thus, this business manager could know all department's every group individual task objectives per week clearly, then who could meet them to attempt to find whether what factors which caused any department's group individual member who could not achieve whose last week objectives efficiently and effectively. The new director seemed have unsuitable personal management style to lead whose different departments to work together to cause their dissatisfaction to him in this KBTZ television station organization. For example, the news department felt this new director lacked leadership ability to led news department managers and associates communicate easily. Moreover, news department associates also complained of very low reward, including pay, promotion opportunities and managerial praise and who also complained of constant criticism , which was the only form of managerial feedback on performance. Hence, it implied the new director did not attempt to solve any departments staffs difficulties to adopt new organization development change to cause their dissatisfaction and conflicts and complaints occurrence to whom. I should suggest this new director as a leader who needed to find method to help different department leader(manager) to lead whose associates to feel this KBTZ organization must earn more beyond the past by providing a rationale for change currently and let them to feel guilt and poor anxiety about this KBTZ organization chose not to change and create a sense of psychological safety to them to concern the change, such as news department associates his complain of low reward, including low promotion opportunities and managerial praise and who also complained of constant criticism feedback on performance. It seemed that who would also complain about low reward, low promotion opportunities and managerial praise and unfair feedback on performance to this new director , even who had good personal managerial style to lead all departments to work. A reason was why these departments, such as news department colleagues complained as above issues because who felt the new director could not adopt to work due to KBTZ sudden change to cause who should be de-commit and dissatisfactory form the status.

Hence, this new director needed to let who to know KBTZ organization would cause poor anxiety and guilt to them in the future if KBTZ organization did not change at this moment as well as this new director might create of psychological discomfort to these departments to let them to know that organization would loss from its television competitions, even it would dismiss who if KBTZ television station should not choose to change at this moment, such as the negative outcomes would be made and KBTZ 's managers and associates would suffer if changes were not made. Moreover, this business manager also needed to remind every department members that as well as who also needed to downward members to know this who individual would need to change to adopt this new organization change culture to every department in large meetings. Even, this new director also needed to let every department manager (leader) to know how this change process needed to carry on and every department manager also needed to implement evaluation systems to track every department's group individual expected behaviours and work performance whether whose work were more efficiently or whose work were not more efficiently during this KBTZ organization was carrying on changing at the same time. Hence, every department manager could create efficient reward systems that reinforce every department's group individual's expected behaviours and who could also ensure that whether the hiring and promotion systems which could support all departments colleagues new demands. Especially, news departments felt low reward dissatisfaction. Hence, it could measure whether who ought to raise reward or who ought not to raise reward of their work performance to evaluate more efficiently and effectively.

In conclusion, When this television broadcast organization needs to expand and develop itself organization to increase many employees to work in different department and improve themselves skills. One efficient organizational development strategy is essential to achieve its organizational development aim in success. This KBTZ organization leader (new director) ought attempt to let all departments staffs to know why it needed to change organization style and what would be the disadvantages to any departments colleagues if it decided not change at this moment. Then, I believed that department

staffs complaints would be reduced and who would feel more fair to pay reward after who knew how who needed to do whose task to adopt this employer to feel satisfactory.

CHAPTER FIVE

Performance management

● Pay structure steps

Human professionals might create the pay structure for their organization, or they might work with an external compensation consultant. There are several steps to design a pay structure: job analysis, job evaluation, pay survey analysis, pay policy and development and pay structure information (Milkovish, G., & Newman, J. 2008).

Milkovich, G. & Newman, J. (2008) explains that the pay structure steps include as below:

Step one : Job analysis is the process of studying jobs in an organization. The outcome of this process is a job description that includes the job title, a summary of the job tasks, adjust of the essential tasks and responsibilities and a description that includes the knowledge, skills and abilities needed to perform the job.

Step two: Job evaluation is the process of judging the relative worth of jobs in an organization. The outcome of job evaluation is the development of an internal structure or hierarchal ranking of jobs. Job-based evaluation is used more often than person-based evaluation and so the former will be the focus in this case. There are three methods of job-based evaluation: The point method, ranking and classification. The job evaluation helps to ensure that pay is internally worth perceived to be fair by employees.

Step three : Pay policy identification is the process of determining whether the organization wants to lead or meet the market in compensation. The pay policy or strategy will likely influence employee attraction. Pay policies can vary across families , i.e. groups of similar jobs, and job level of the top management feels that different areas of the organization.

Step four: Pay survey analysis is the process of analysising compensation data gathered from other employers in a survey of the relevant labor market. Gathering external data , e.g. base pay, bonuses , stock or share options and benefits is the essential to keep the organization's compensation externally competitive within the industry. Employee attraction can be improved by maintaining externally pay structures.

Step five: Pay structure creation is the final step, in which the internal structure (step two of job evaluation) is combined with the external market pay rates . Step four: Pay survey analysis in a simple regression to develop a market pay line. Depending on whether the organization wants to lead or meet the market, the market pay line can be adjusted top or down. To complete the pay structure , pay grades and pay ranges are developed.

In this organization's job analysis, it can influence these positions or job titles. For example, office support department has the lower level, front line receptionist, middle level, admin. assistant and top level, assistant to the director of operations. Operations department has the lower level, operations trainee, operations trainee, middle level , operations analyst, top level, director of regional operations, top level, director of regional operations. Human resource department has the lower level, payroll assistant, the middle level, benefits counselor and benefits manager, the top level, HR director.

In this organization, the administrative assistants, perform similar administrative tasks across departments and do not handle function-specific tasks , e.g. HR. Thus, this organization's administrative assistant ought be suggested grouping the front-line administrative jobs in a separate job family called office support. However, in some organizations, administrative assistant has possible to need to handle function-specific tasks, e.g. HR. Hence, in these organizations administrative assistant can be the low level group to HR department.

In the job evaluation step, this organization chooses to apply point method to evaluate the pay worth to every job title. The evaluation points method can be weights for example the four degrees for education level are identified as below:

1=high school, 2=assocaites, 3= bacholors, 4=master/graduate points are then calculated by multiplying the degree by the weights.

The compensable factor for the evaluation for front desk reception as below:

skill (50%) degree(1,2,3,4) weight points
education level 1 25% 25
degree of

technical skills 1 25% 25
responsibility(30%)
scope of control 1 10% 10
impact of job 2 20% 40
degree of
problem solving 1 10% 10
task complexity 1 10% 10
120

The ensure that the pay structure is extremely competitive, a pay survey will be conducted. The market pay data must be from the relevant labor market. Surveys can include i.e. six organizations who recruit and hire similar jobs in the regions. Base pay salary data from the responding organizations are reflected to ensure the summary job descriptions , sample data are appropriately similar to those in this organization in order to compare and analyze the pay data between other similar organizations and this organization.

Finally , it need to implement how to design the pay structure. it can be settled the pay ranges for each pay grade, pay ranges create upper and lower pay rates for each job in the pay scale. Each pay grade will have a minimum and maximum pay rate. It is important to remember that all jobs in a paygrade will have the same minimum and maximum pay rates. Percent guidelines below the midpoint the pay range will reach . For example, the maximum might be 10% percent above the midpoint and the minimum might be 10% below the midpoint. The percent guidelines can be based on input from the organization's job evaluation committee, e.g. clerical and office positions: 10% above and below the midpoint. Enter to mid-level professional and management positions: 30 % above and below the midpoint.

● What is key performance indicator (KPI) components?

Performance management strategy of performance metrics are a powerful tool of organizational change. It can measure organizational performance really. Companies define objectives , establish goals, measure progress, reward achievement, and display the results for all productivity. Executives can use performance metrics to define and communicate strategic objectives tailor to every individual and role in the organization. Managers can use them to identify forming individuals or teams and guide them and employees can use performance metrics to focus on what is important and help them achieve goal defined in their personal performance plans.

But wrong metrics can have unintended consequences: They can threaten to prolong on organizational processes, demoralize employees and undermine productivity and service levels. If the metrics do not accurately translate the company's strategy and goals into real useful actions that employees can take on a daily basis. Employees will work hard but have nothing to show for their efforts, everyone will feel tired and frustrated, also the company will be efficient but ineffective.

Performance metrics are a critical ingredient of performance management, performance management has a four steps cycle involves strategize misson, value, goals, objectives, incentives, strategy maps. Then, it needs to plan budgets, forecasts, models, targets. Next , it needs to monitor / analyze performance report, analytical tools. Finally, it needs to adjust or make action to assess, decide and track in execution step.

A performance metrics measurement tool can fasten the business, distill an organization's strategy to serve its stakeholders, linking strategy to processes. A performance metrics can give visual information delivery system that lets users measure, monitor, and manage the effectiveness of their tactics and their progress toward achieving strategic objectives . Collecting , a performance metrics measurement tool enable users to identify problems and opportunities, taken action and adjust plans and goals as needed.

What is key performance indicator (KPI) components? The only difference between a metric and KPA is that a KPI is a strategic objective and measures performance against a goal. KPI is a strategic objective , KPI measure performance against specific targets. Targets are defined in strategic planning, or budget sessions and can take different forms , e.g. achievement, reduction, absolute zero, targets have ranges of performance, e.g. above on, or below target. Targets are assigned time frame by which they must be accomplished. Time frame is often divided into smaller intervals, targets are measured against a baseline or benchmark. The previous year's results often serve as a benchmark.

The goals associated with KPIs are known as targets because they specify a measuerble outcome rather then a conceptual destination. Ideally, executives, managers and workers collectively set targets during strategic planning or budget discussions.

In performance management view point, target can be defined five types: Achievement means performance should reach or exceed the target. Anything over the target is valuable but not required, e.g. revenue and satisfaction. Reduction means performance should reach or be lower than the target. Anything less than the target is value, but not required, e.g. absolute means performance should equal the target. Anything above or below is not good, e.g. in-stock percentage and on time delivery. Minimum/ maximum means performance should be within a range of value. Anything above or below the range is not good , e.g. mean time between repairs, zero means performance should equal zero, which is the minimum value possible, e.g. employee injuries and product defects. All above these target will be key performance indicator performance tool.

For time frames example, performance targets have time frames, which affects hoe KPIs are calculated and displayed. Many organizations establish annul targets for key processes. To keep employees on track to achieve those long -term targets, many organizations divide time frames into intervals, that are measured on a more frequent basis. For example, a group may divide the annual target to improve customer satisfaction from 60% to 68% into four quarterly inter with 2% target improvement each quarter. However, in some cases, such as a retail environment is affected by seasonal shopping, groups many back weighs. The targets toward the end of the year, since most holiday season, during the Dec. holiday season.

Finally, KPI targets could be measured against a benchmark that becomes the starting point for improving performance . Typically, the benchmark is last year's output. So, for example, a sales team may need to increase sales by 20% compared to last year. Or the benchmark could be an external standard , such as the performance level of an industry leader. So, a company might want to set a goals of closing the gap in market share with its closet competitor by 50% next year.

Users can read KPIs to look at a visual display that has been properly encoded and know whether a process of project is on track. To assist users can understand KPI (key performance indicator) performance measurement more easily. It has seven attributes for each. They include: status measures performance against the target and is usually shown with a stoplight. Trend measures performance against the prior interval or another time period and is often displayed using arrows or trend lines. The actual and target values are self-explanatory and usually displayed with text. Variance measures the gap between actual and target and is displayed using text or a micro bar chart in performance report variance percentage divides the variance against the target. These seven attributes can combine to provide valuable insight into the state of performance.

● How to Implement a Performance Management System

Depending on what kind of changes have been made we will have to prepare a communication and change management plan in order to transfer the organization smoothly from one to another PMS. While the small changes can be covered by simple communication informing about the changes in the system, major changes may even require change of mindset and old habits, which will need a more serious change management plan.

It is a system that is linked to and feeds many other HR tolls and systems meaning that the final results of those tools are highly dependent on the inputs that they get from the PMS. Having that kind of importance and influence this system, though complex in its nature, from one side has to be as simple as possible so that all managers can willingly and easily use it, while on the other side it has to offer quality results that can be used as inputs for the other HR tools and systems.

The quality of the system and the results it offers depend on the process of setting up the system itself. Doing a good job in planning, defining and introducing the system will do half of the job in securing quality results from the system. So how do we set up a Performance Management System? Implementation of a Performance Management System is a project of its own... as every other project it needs serious approach towards all project elements and phases.

The implementation of a Performance Management System is a project of its own so it should be treated as one. So, as every other project of this character it needs serious approach towards all project elements and phases such as defining, planning, people, resource and stakeholder management, implementation, monitoring, measuring etc..

The performance management system may contain all of these components, but it is the overall system that matters, not the individual components. Many organizations have been able to develop effective performance management systems without all of the following practices.

A performance management system includes the following actions:

•Develop clear job descriptions using an employee recruitment plan that identifies the selection team.

•Recruit potential employees and select the most qualified to participate in interviews onsite.

•Conduct interviews to narrow down your pool of candidates.

•Hold multiple additional meetings, as needed, to get to know your candidates' strengths, weaknesses, and abilities to contribute what you need. Use potential employee testing and assignments where they make sense for the position that you are filling.

•Select appropriate people using a comprehensive employee selection process to identify the most qualified candidate who has the best cultural fit and job fit that you need.

•Offer your selected candidate the job and negotiate the terms and conditions of employment including salary, benefits, paid time off, and other organizational perks.

•Welcome the new employee to your organization.

•Provide effective new employee orientation, assign a mentor, and integrate your new employee into the organization and its culture.

•Negotiate requirements and accomplishment-based performance standards, outcomes, and measures between the employee and his or her new manager.

•Provide ongoing education and training as needed.

•Provide on-going coaching and feedback.

•Conduct quarterly performance development planning discussions.

•Design effective compensation and recognition systems that reward people for their ongoing contributions.

•Provide promotional/career development opportunities including lateral moves, transfers, and job shadowing for staff.

•Assist with exit interviews to understand WHY valued employees leave the organization.

•Performance Appraisals Don't Work tells you why you want to move away from the traditional appraisal system.

•Performance Management Glossary Entry provides a basic definition of performance management.

•Performance Management Is Not an Annual Appraisal provides the components of a performance management system.

•Performance Management Process Checklist gives you the components of the performance management process.

•Performance Development Planning provides the steps for preparing and implementing performance development planning.

•Performance Development Planning Form is used to write out specific goals and measurements, to be updated quarterly.

•Goal Setting: Beyond Traditional SMART Goals discusses goal setting.

•Tips to Help Managers Improve Performance Appraisals provides concrete suggestions about how those of you who have to manage in a traditional performance appraisal culture can make them better—for both you and the employee.

•Common Problems With Performance Appraisals identifies the most common reasons why appraisals are not effective.

•Phrases for Approaching Performance Reviews and Difficult Conversations shares tips about successfully holding a comfortable appraisal meeting.

Finally, performance appraisal is one part of performance management system. The process by which a manager or consultant (1) examines and evaluates an employee's work behavior by comparing it with preset standards, (2) documents the results of the comparison, and (3) uses the results to provide feedback to the employee to show where improvements are needed and why. Performance appraisals are employed to determine who needs what training, and who will be promoted, demoted, retained, or fired.

● Performance management aim

Performance management means the goal of reward programs are to attract, motivate people and it is essential for the company to clearly identify the performance and competency levels required of their employees in different roles at different levels. The company will then evaluate , differentiate and reward the employees in a fair and consistent way.

Performance management is one of the most important functions in human resource management. It is also an important tool to link individual objectives with departmental targets. It is a part of a comprehensive human resource management strategy. It needs to let objectives into practical and realistic performance goals at each level of the company. It provides employees clear aims and forms on job expectation motivates employees to perform better, helps focus on the desired results, improves communication, helps develop employees, capabilities and helps achieve organizational objectives.

It's elements include : planning means agreement on performance goals and targets, based on job descriptions and business objectives, goals and targets have to be specific to clear, measurable, specify quantity, quality, time, money etc., achievable to solve challenges, but within each of competent and committed person, relevant to the company's objectives. So, that the individual's goals can contribute towards the company's objective, monitoring and coaching means on ongoing and continuous process, monitor performance against agreed goals and targets, provide direction/ support and feedback on how well people are doing, recognize and reinforce desirable behaviours, coach and help solve difficulties in achieving desirable performance, identify problem at early stage, take corrective action in a timely manner.

Then, performance review or appraisal meeting means that it is a formal review on the individual's performance, it is usually done once or twice a year to review, monitor and employees for promotion, help identify the training and development needs of employees, achieve a better two way communication between the line manager and the employee with regards to performance.

Next, preparation for the appraisal meeting, it is necessary to keep a record of the individual's performance and achievement with gives support to rating, allow sufficient time for preparation on, what performance problems are to be mentioned, views on the possible reasons for success or failure, any suggestions to solve the problem, give sufficient notice to employee regarding the meeting and respect employee to have a self-appraisal before the meeting they can identify their own achievements and problems. Finally preparation of the appraisal form, it should be as simple and brief as possible and allow sufficient time for comments, terms should be easily understood, with some notes for guidance, information to collect on the form includes: Key result areas, agreed objectives/targets , assessment of performance against the key result area details of the development plan to improve performance.

What are the development activities participated for current appraisal period mean? Review the development activities are participated by the employee for the past appraisal period and to agree on a development plan for the coming appraisal period. Management coaching for performance means that managers and supervisors have an important role to play in performance management, which is to provide feedback and coaching on employee's performance when necessary, coaching is a process that helps the employee gain how to win overcome barriers to improve job performance on a as need basis, when training uses a structured design to provide the employees with the knowledge and skills to perform a task.

The other difference between coaching and training is that the former is normally done in real time. That is , it is performed on the job, at the workplace. The coach uses real-life tasks and problems to help the learners increase their performance. Otherwise, training and learning is taught to a group students to learn in a coaching is effective when it is specific to the individual and it is positive and it is positive and occurs as soon as performance problems are identifies.

Coaching for individual benefit performance includes to identify performance problem by pointing out the facts/describing the behaviours observed in a professional manner, support with evidence if possible, clarify the expectations/standards of the job, explain the consequence of inappropriate actions/behaviours, ask for the employee's view point and how they assess their own actions/behaviours , discuss the causes of the problem/analyze reasons for sub-standard performance, develop and agree on solutions, decide on specific action(s) to be taken.

Why is reward communication important? for this case, a company could be wasting the money spent on salaries and benefits by leaving employees when they listen the true value of the total package. Without employee understanding, reward programs won't motivate employee effort reward achieving business objectives. So, effective reward communication can let candidates existing staff appreciate or understand the value of the retirement scheme or other benefits, such as subsidized meals, life insurance and critical illness insurance. However, if rewards are used to motivate employees, or to encourage higher performance aims, it is essential to have an effective communicating information about pay scales, the provision of benefits and allowances, grading systems, job evaluation , performance-related pay schemes and how pay decisions and made for different individuals or groups of employees.

In conclusion, performance management is not an annual appraisal meeting. It is not preparing for that appraisal meeting nor is it a self-evaluation. It's not a form nor is it a measuring tool although many organizations may use tools and forms to track goals and improvements, they are not the process of performance management.

Note: Performance management is the process of creating a work environment or setting in which people are enabled to perform to the best of their abilities.

Performance management is a whole work system that begins when a job is defined as needed. It ends when an employee leaves your organization. Performance management defines your interaction with an employee at every step of the way in between these major life cycle occurrences. Performance management makes every interaction opportunity with an employee into a learning occasion.

Performance management aims at building a high performance culture for both the individuals and the teams so that they jointly take the responsibility of improving the business processes on a continuous basis and at the same time raise the competence bar by upgrading their own skills within a leadership framework. Its focus is on enabling goal clarity for making people do the right things in the right time. It may be said that the main objective of a performance management system is to achieve the capacity of the employees to the full potential in favor of both the employee and the organization, by defining the expectations in terms of roles, responsibilities and accountabilities, required competencies and the expected behaviors.

The main goal of performance management is to ensure that the organization as a system and its subsystems work together in an integrated fashion for accomplishing optimum results or outcomes.

The major objectives of performance management are discussed below:

?To enable the employees towards achievement of superior standards of work performance.

?To help the employees in identifying the knowledge and skills required for performing the job efficiently as this would drive their focus towards performing the right task in the right way.

?Boosting the performance of the employees by encouraging employee empowerment, motivation and implementation of an effective reward mechanism.

?Promoting a two way system of communication between the supervisors and the employees for clarifying expectations about the roles and accountabilities, communicating the functional and organizational goals, providing a regular and a transparent feedback for improving employee performance and continuous coaching.

?Identifying the barriers to effective performance and resolving those barriers through constant monitoring, coaching and development interventions.

?Creating a basis for several administrative decisions strategic planning, succession planning, promotions and performance based payment.

?Promoting personal growth and advancement in the career of the employees by helping them in acquiring the desired knowledge and skills.

Some of the key concerns of a performance management system in an organization are:

?Concerned with the output (the results achieved), outcomes, processes required for reaching the results and also the inputs (knowledge, skills and attitudes).

?Concerned with measurement of results and review of progress in the achievement of set targets.

?Concerned with defining business plans in advance for shaping a successful future.

?Striving for continuous improvement and continuous development by creating a learning culture and an open system.

?Concerned with establishing a culture of trust and mutual understanding that fosters free flow of communication at all levels in matters such as clarification of expectations and sharing of information on the core values of an organization which binds the team together.

?Concerned with the provision of procedural fairness and transparency in the process of decision making.

The performance management approach has become an indispensable tool in the hands of the corporates as it ensures that the people uphold the corporate values and tread in the path of accomplishment of the ultimate corporate vision and mission. It is a forward looking process as it involves both the supervisor and also the employee in a process of joint planning and goal setting in the beginning of the year.

● What is the difference between performance management and performance appraisal?

Performance appraisals are one of the crucial aspects of professionally managed organizations across the world. Each organization has set an appraisal system in place in order to raise its employees' performance over a period of time. They are based on a review of the performance of an employee on the tasks assigned to it. They are used for many aspects such as salary revision, bonus provisions, promotions etc. These reviews are mostly conducted annually, but may be considered quarterly or half-yearly as well depending upon the HR policies of the organizations. Mostly, Human Resource department takes the lead in conducting formal performance appraisals.

Otherwise, performance management systems are set in place to guide the employees to achieve a desired level of performance. It is basically a definition of what organization expects from employee over the next appraisal period. Specific objectives are set for short term (say next quarter), and employee is prepared to achieve the desired outcomes by meeting these short term targets. These targets are defined by the job description along with the desired outcome of the jobs. This helps employees to determine the gaps in their performance and thus helps them to improve before the final performance appraisal happens after a year or six months. However, performance management aims at overall personal development of the employees. It is a form of constructive feedback which encourages continuous improvement. It is helpful to both employee as well as appraiser. There is frequent communication between them which helps in setting right goals for the employee and possible guidelines from appraiser to achieve those goals in an effective manner. It therefore saves employees from the bitter feeling that comes at year end when they feel that they have wasted one whole year without any substantial value addition.

● What are performance management system

The common goals of performance management system consider our daily work routine about our purpose in an organization. It is important to let organizational members understand what their organizations' visions and goals are, how their work fits into the organization, and how they contribute to their mission accomplishment. Hence one effective performance management system can encourage and improve the organization's members to raise their effort to contribute to their organizations. So, it brings this question: How to design one effective performance management system?

A clear understanding of job expectations is needed. When employees and supervisors have a clear understanding of their specific job duties in the workforce are eliminated. Each employee will be expect to contribute their own duties and responsibilities efficiently. All effective performance management system can empower employees to think about and clarify every employee's role in the organization. Organizations need to set clear goals and expectations to help with them. Employee performance plans must provide for balanced, credible measuring expected results, the performance plans include results, the performance plans include appropriate resources, such as quality, quantity, timeliness, and/or cost-effectiveness. Moreover, performance expectations must be based on job analysis and understandable, reasonable and attainable and clear specific.

Regular feedback facilitates better communication in the workplace factor is important. Performance strengths and weaknesses. How can employee individual performance can get improvement? In fact, performance management can be a motivational tool, when this tool can let employees to feel more satisfactory. Then, the supervisors can have a performance feedback process that facilitates between the supervisors and their employees. Hence, performance feedback ought need to be regular feedback facilitated better communication in the workplace. It can reduce from normal pressures of work.

How to design effective performance management system ? AN effective management system can measure organizational and employee performance. Performance management involves multiple levels of analysis, and is clearly linked to the topics studied in strategy HRM as well as performance appraisal. The objectives of performance management system often include motivating performance, helping individuals, developing their skills, building a performance culture, determining who should be promoted, eliminating individuals who are poor performers, and helping implement strategies.

Hence, the main purposes of a performance include: The work is performed the best by employees, employees have a clear understanding of the quality of work expected from them, employees effectively these are performing relative to expectation, awards and salary increases based on employee performance are distributed, opportunity for employee development and finding reasons and solutions why the employee performance that does not need expectation. These issues will be performance management usually main purposes.

However, performance management system usually have these phases: Phase 1 (developing and planning performance) , It includes outline development plans, setting objectives and getting commitment for the organization. Phase 2 (managing and review performance), it includes assess against objectives, feedback, coaching , document reviews, . Phase 3 (reward performance) , it includes personal development, link to pay , results performance. What is the performance management aim? On setting objectives stage, the management needs to know how to achieve and help to encourage commitment and understanding by linking. The employees' work with the organization's goals and objectives. It needs to let employees to know how to achieve its missions clearly. So, targets need to be settled for each performance and goals setting is the fundamental aspect for an organization. They further indicated that productivity gains will be supported for and employees' participation in the process of setting objectives. It is a motivational process which also gives the individual the feeling of being involved and creates a sense of ownership for employees.

In management and review stage, this involves maintaining a positive approach to work, updating and revising initial objectives, performance standard and job competency areas as conditions change, requesting feedback from a supervisor, providing feedback to supervisors, suggesting career development experiences, employees and supervisors working together, managing the performance management process.

Hence, performance needs to be compared. It is between desired performance and actual performance. When they are measured , then they will give feedback and development. Then, feedback will five opinions to desired performance in order to make performance revision again, even again. Finally, when the desired performance can be achieved the best actual performance measurement result and it will bring actual performance development to achieve actual vision, mission, strategy, value drivers consequently.

IN the rewarding performance, it has three activities: personnel development, linking to pay and identifying the results or performance. In fact, all personnel development is basically self-development. Opportunity for development is valuable only if the individual capitalizes on himself/ herself. Development should be designed to improve performance on the current job and then prepare the employee for promotion. In fact, it is only the employees who get promoted , who are currently doing outstanding work and this have been able to demonstrate their capacity to assume greater responsibilities. Furthermore, training activities should ideally to based on performance gaps that are identified during the performance review phase.

So, regular performance feedbacks are important factors to influence skills development. In addition organizations need a growing interest in pay-for -performance plans focused on small groups or teams. Small group pays provide monetary rewards based on the measured performance of the group or team. However, high performing, effective organizations have a culture that encourages employee involvement. Therefore, employees are more willing to get involved in decision-making, goal setting or problem solving activities, which subsequently result in higher employee performance.

Thus, one effective performance management system needs to follow these steps to implement, such as developing and planning performance step: it includes to set what the main objectives , the organization needs. Then it is managing and review performance step, the organizations need to review whether what differences are between its desired performance and actual performance to prepare review their performance difference. Next, it is reward management implementation, the organization needs to give better record to the talent employees in order to encourage they develop their skills in the maximum effort as well as it also needs to punish the poor performance employees in order to expect they can review their error. In consequence, all these steps must be followed step by step to implement the performance management system effectively.

Reference
Milkovich, G., & Newman, J. (2008). Compensation, MC Graw-Hill Irwin. 0*NET. Available at http:// online.onetcenter.org
● Performance management strategy raises bank organization efficiency

● What role influences personality play in the time pressure bank working situation ? Can performance management strategy solve different departments employees efficiencies, in front line service and back line support service bank organizations ?

Personality is a stable set of characteristics representing the internal properties of an individual. These characteristics, or traits are relatively, are major determinants of behaviour and influence behaviour across a wide variety of situation. The personality played role in the situation at the bank as: Marian, new employee of this bank loan manager, although she had more experienced in bank loan department, but she could not deal how to persuade this bank eight sections of managers to discuss how to solve loan volumes decreasing trouble successfully and meeting was poor performance and these was no result within eight months. Finally, she decided to enquire Vince Stoddard, the bank president to give suggestion to her how to persuade them to attend any meeting and how to persuade Dave, loan manager to assist her. Hence, she could not perform that she was one experienced person to have ability to solve any staffs personal trouble in this bank loan department within eight months successfully. I think she had an emotional instability trait, the degree to her to handle this issue stressful and she handled high demand situation with difficult. It influenced her job performance poorly and she could not success to work with this bank loan eight sections of managers ,so she could not feel job satisfaction. Her lower levels of emotional instability tended to be negative due to she needed to find bank president to help her to solve this staff meeting trouble easily and she could not attempt to solve staff meeting to discuss how to increase loan volumes by herself within these eight months. Dave, the bank old loan manager and other seven sections of loan managers, whose personalities were non-agreeableness trait. Agreeableness is the degree to which a person is easy going and tolerant, who believes in the honesty of others, willing to help others and not tend to make conflict and is sensitive to the feelings of others. Due these bank eight sections of loan managers who did not like to attend meeting with Marian to discuss how to solve loan volumes decreasing trouble and there were no any solutions and Dave, this bank old loan manager who does not like to assist Marian to solve this trouble. Thus, I think they are non-agreeableness trait to play in the situation at this bank.

● suggestion of performance management method to reduce time working pressure in different bank departments

Which the big five personality traits most clearly influenced Marian and Dave when they feel time pressure reducing to work together in the bank?

The big five personality dimensions and the job satisfaction to staffs which have close relationship. Individuals have stable traits that significantly influence their affective and behavioural reactions to organizational settings. Generally, employees who are high in openness, conscientiousness to be more satisfied with their job. Job satisfaction means a pleasurable or a positive emotional stable resulting from the appraisal of one's job or job experience. How the big five personality traits influence job satisfaction and to be able to derive recommendations an recruitment, selection and placement of employees. It relies on factors such as co-workers, promotions and salaries as the only factors that may have an impact on job satisfaction. But the individual difference which is the personality of an individual. It can affect job satisfaction. It assumes that when an individual is in a job situation that suits whose personality who is more satisfied. Personality traits can be described in terms of five basic factors, which are extraversion, agreeableness, conscientiousness, neuroticism and openness to experience job satisfaction relationship of personality traits. In terms of applying personality to the personal environment fit conceptualization , it is important to consider that certain jobs and job tasks require different personality traits. A job which involves a great deal of interpersonal relations may require an individual to be agreeable and extraverted in order to perform at a high level. For example, individuals who are extraverted may have a strong ability to deal with job tasks of an interpersonal nature. If individuals are high on a given personality trait, they will have a preference for job characteristics which are in live with this personality trait. If these preferences are matched with the characteristics of the job, a high characteristics will then activate the relevant personality traits and this activation will lead to increased motivation and therefore result in increased job performance and job satisfaction. In contrast a low satisfactory personal environment fit is likely to result in dissatisfaction and ultimately leaving the occupation. For example, in the banking sectors employees hold different positions. These may include tellers, tellers' supervisors, customer service and sales consultants, branch and assistant managers, loan officers and clerks. This model can be forced on how personality affects job satisfaction . Hence, the personal environment fit suggests that these be a match between individual's personality and the positions they occupy.To give a general view or assumption, it can be said that an effective loan officer or bank teller must have an extraverted personality, as extroverts are warm, exhibit positive emotions and are sociable, hence,who perform well in sociable environments. On banking loan consultants may have a low neuroticism personality, as low neurotic individuals are self confidents and tolerant to stress, hence, it helps them to build credibility and trust with clients. Also, one may say that bank loan department managerial positions, as Marian and Dave may require an individual who is high on agreeableness traits , as who are concerned with others' well being. Hence, they create fair environment and overall one can stay in all positions individuals may have a conscientiousness personality , as this provides for aiming for achievement, acting dutifully being. organized and efficient. Therefore, personality affects how individuals gain satisfaction with their work.

The big five personality traits which most clearly influenced Marian and Dave include that: For example, in the case of bank employee loan manager, Marian and Dave who have an extraversion personality will be satisfied as whose job allows who to be friendly and communicate directly with whose clients. Therefore, one can agree that personality has an effect on the way individuals perform whose work. For another example, if a person has a openness personality trait who will look for work which allows for innovation and creative thinking, such as being an artist or working in formation technology. In conclusion, due to bank is a bank offering financial services to clients industry. Hence, employees' personalities and job satisfaction can influence bank productivity and service quality directly as well as the big five personality traits which are neuroticism, agreeableness, openness, conscientiousness and extraversion of every employee personal characteristics are absolutely related to influence how their work behaviour and attitude to serve their bank client.

● Which of the cognitive and motivational aspects of personality played at role when bank staffs can feel time pressure reducing by performance management strategy ?

The personal environment fit theory has been identified as a way of studying the fit between the job characteristics and the abilities and needs of the individual holding the job. Job satisfaction, organizational commitment, career commitment and career satisfaction are significantly stable over time. Thus, it is possible that what causes individuals to feel satisfied or dissatisfied within themselves. The concept of the personal environment fit basically indicates characteristics of people and their environment results in a positive outcome for both individual and organization.This may mean that a good fit may lead to organization effectiveness and high performance at the same time employees will be satisfied with their work which leads to self actualization and lower stress levels.

Working within the bounds of her personality, what should Marian have done when trouble first seemed to the brewing when she can feel time pressure reducing?

Personality is defined as those feelings, thought, desires and tendencies toward behaviour that contribute to a person's individuality. Marian personality should seem to be the kind of person who did not know how to solve any problem independently . She was usually in control of her behaviour , but it was not easy to control her internal emotion. She knew her emotion reaction to report of executive office when she found any unsatisfactory behaviours from her colleagues and she would be free to think about the problem and made a decision about solving it immediately. It could be found these issues from her past behaviours. For example, she had joined bank eight months ago, as a manager in charge of eight loan sections.

In fact, bank loan volumes were still decreasing during Marian had worked in the bank eight months. Although, she had attempt to call a staff meeting with all of the eight loan section managers, she began to explain that loan volumes were reducing to let them to know to help her to solve this issue, but even, then each subsequent meetings were poor and did not improve. Finally, she asked Vince Stoddard bank president to help her to attempt how to solve staff meeting trouble, but he hadn't been very friendly to give suggestion to her to solve. Otherwise, he was waiting for her to take solution. Hence, Marian should have done foolish behaviour to enquire Vince Stoddard president to help her to solve staff meeting trouble, she could not attempt to solve independently. This issue influenced Vince Stoddard president felt that she was not an experienced and good ability loan manager to help whose bank to achieve to increase loan application volumes successfully.

● How should she have maintained Dave's job satisfaction and commitment when she can let Dave can feel less time pressure to work in bank? Does this bank lack performance management to cause employees feel working time pressure and influence working performance efficiencies ?

Personality refers to the totality an individual's behavioural and emotional characteristic, moods, attitude, options, motivations and style of thinking, perceiving, speaking and acting. Personality influences how others interact with individuals and how they evaluate and reward or punish them . Hence, personality affects how individuals experience work events to feel job satisfaction and commitment from their employer. Job satisfaction defined the extent to which employees like their work. It includes the employees like their work. It includes the different aspects of the jobs , such as promotion, opportunities or relation to colleagues. Lack of job satisfaction among employees lead to less productivity, low employee retention, high absenteeism and low morale. A lack of job satisfaction resulting in a low level of employee commitment, impact on performance and the achievement of organizational goals. Low job satisfaction may result in low productivity, high absenteeism, labour unrest and industrial action and high labour turnover. There is a relation between personality and job satisfaction among bank employees. Bank organizations in recruiting, selecting and placing of employees in their jobs , who will be a person job fit to avoid dissatisfaction. Job satisfaction influences an organization's well being with regard to job productivity, employee turnover, absenteeism and life satisfaction. Therefore it is crucial to understand how personality traits affects job satisfaction to improve the selection, recruitment and placing processes in organizations. It also helps individuals to choose their field of study with an understand of their personality to avoid dissatisfaction as it impacts negatively on their working lives.

These aspects of employees feeling to this bank is very important to cause their service attitude to clients and work efficiency, job satisfaction aspect , such as remuneration, promotion, work and supervision relationship. Hence, Marian ought attempt to let Dave to feel they are the working partnership (loan manager partners) relationship and are not the work and supervision relationship. It can be concluded that in order for Marian's new bank employer to be successful in their operation. She must be equipped with quality personnel and able to provide good services to the clients. In this ever increasingly, competitive, complex and challenging business environment, this bank needs to ensure it retains its current , profitable old loan applicant clients (increase new loan application customers retention) in order to survive support and loyalty from clients are ensured through acceptable client service. Hence, Marian ought have openness and agreeableness attitude to invite this bank loan department Dave manager and other managers to enquire them why who have no time to attend her meeting regularly individually in her room and she also ought attempt to give some suggestions to them how to increase loan application client numbers. Hence, her one to one individual meeting can avoid who indicate having none any time reason to attend regular meeting together again and she can make Dave , this bank manager feel she doesn't need he assists her and she can deal this difficult issue independently to her employer. I recommend that Marian, this bank new loan department manager, who ought attempt to change Dave, this bank old loan department manager's working attitude to make him to have more job satisfaction and commitment. She aims to encourage he can attempt to increase his confidence to lead his loan department team to increase further loan applicant numbers and making him to feel that Dave is a experienced loan manager and only he has ability to assist Marian how to solve loan application volumes decreasing and increasing payment problem.

● How should Marian proceed now that the situation has become very difficult to be improved less time pressure working environment when the bank does not implement good performance management strategy?

Generally, banks offer five main categories of services, namely cash accessibility, asset security, money transfers , loans and financial advice . Marian will work in this loans and financial advice department in this bank. Banks need to make asset security to their clients through safes and by securing the safety of money deposits. Money transfers refer to the banking service of moving clients funds from one account to another, including payment services to external parties. A bank needs to provide the service of loans to its clients.lastly, banks provide financial advice, including advice on investments, wills, taxation, leasing, mergers and personal financial planning. Hence, loan lending service is among of one aspect of bank service to its clients.This bank exists problems of loan applicant numbers were reducing and loan department staffs did not like to go to meeting regularly. It was possible that who felt client numbers are decreasing to lend loans from this bank. It was not serious to influence their job performance directly. They could cause ability to be similar to a team cooperation to threaten Marian , new loan manager to force them to go to attend meeting regularly.

Marian needs to consider change management of this bank loan department manager, Dave's personality and team leadership skill. Her changing must be realistic, achievable and measurable. Before, Marian decided to work in this bank loan department manager position first day in the high time pressure working environement. Marian needed to ask her these questions:

What did she want to achieve with this change?

Why and how would she know that the change has been achieved?

Who was affected by this change?

How would they react to it?

How much of the bank loan department change could it achieve loan volumes increasing outcome?

What parts of her change did she need help with?

She needed to consider this issues because these aspects related strongly to her management of personality to Dave loan manager as well as whether loan volumes could be increased from her leadership. Psychological contract theory, which helps to explain the complex relationship between an organization and its employees. However, Marian ,the new bank loan manager has responsibility for managing change, the employee doesn't have a responsibility to manage change because Dave's responsibility is no other than to do whose best, which is different for every loan department managers and depends on a wide variety of factors (health, maturity, stability, experience, personality, motivation etc). Her responsibility for managing her bank loan department change is with management and executives of her bank loan application increasing volumes and organizational department and she must manage her bank loan department change in a way that all loan department managers can cope with it. Hence, she has a responsibility to facilitate and enable her bank loan department and then to help her loan department all eight section managers to understand reasons and aims to ways of responding positively according to every team of loan manager's own situation and capabilities. Increasingly every loan manager's role is to interpret, communicate and enable, not to instruct and impose which nobody really responds to well. Her change includes mindset change and changing people's mindsets or changing attitudes, because it often indicates a tendency towards imposed or enforced change (theory X) and it implies strongly that her new bank employer's loan department believes that its loan department managers and loan consultants and loan clerks etc staffs currently have the wrong mindset. If these staffs were not approaching their tasks or their loan organizational department effectively, then the loan department has the wrong mindset, not the staffs. Changing is such as new structures, policies, targets, re-locations, etc all create bank new systems and working environment, which need to be explained to her loan department staffs as early as possible, so that her loan department staffs' validating and refining the changes themselves can be obtained.

Whenever, the bank new loan employee manager, Marian , her loan department imposes new things on her staffs, there will be difficulties. Participation, involvement and open easily, full communication are the important factors.Thus, if Marian hoped to change hew new bank employer eight loan managers, included Dave manager whose every personal attitude successfully, she needed involve and agree support from these staffs within system (system means environment, processes, culture, relationships, behaviours etc), whether personal or loan organizational department) ; she needed to understand where she and her bank loan department was at the moment and she also needed to understand where she wanted to be, when, why and what the measures would be for having got there; her plans development to loan department e.g. job reorganization, task analysis, job transfer due to information technological development or outsourcing etc which needed to toward in an appropriate achievable measurable stages and she needed to communicate, involve, enable and facilitate involvement from her loan department all staffs as early and openly and as fully as is possible. Marian, she is as a leader (manager) in her new employer, bank loan department to anticipate with eight sections of loan managers to discuss loan decreasing volumes issue. She ought not to be an autocratic leader to use strong, directive, laissez faire actions to enforce the rules, regulations and relationships in her work environment. She ought be a path-goal leader , she needs to select the most appropriate style from directive style or supportive style participative style or achievement oriented style to help her loan department managers and consultants, clerks etc different position staffs (followers) to clarify the paths that lead them to work and achieve personal goals.Hence, loan department every staffs are assigned to positions to allocate whose authority and responsibility, depending on qualifications are assessed by examination or training and working experience fairly. It aims to build their confidence to continue to serve their current bank employer.

● Performance management strategy solve Puma finance service corporation organization finance salespeople service performance

How time pressure influences the finance service compensation director behavior when he feel time pressure to manage his finance team how to sell their finance package to new clients attractively in short time?

Frances Mead , compensation director for Puma corporation , who paid well to hire Don Coggin to fill position of benefits administrator for her company in corporate personnel department at Puma, headquartered in Salt Lake city, Utah and the job was located in Utah. Hence, Don could always enjoyed the outdoor and he liked to backpack, camp and did some mountain climbing sport entertainment conveniently. Hence, it ensured that this job location could give Dan to enjoy his likely mountain climbing ,camp, backpack sport entertainment conveniently was also an important reason to influence Don to choose this job.In fact, Dan's financial background aided him greatly in his new benefits administrator job, where he was responsible for development and administration of the pension plan, life and health insurance package, employee stock purchase plan and other employee benefit programs within one month. Dan has learned how to do duties. Frances Mead, she was satisfied with her selection for Dan to do this benefits administrator position. Hence, she expected Dan to move up to in the department rank rapidly, but Dan only concern was that who did not seem to have enough time to enjoy his outdoor activities after he had seem promoted to do further duties absolutely. It implied that Dan disliked to promote to spend more time to do more job duties.

Even, his salary would not be increased and his rank would be promoted in this moment. After six months, Dan had his job proficiently and who was quite talented and the job did not present a strong challenge to him. During to Frances, compensation director for Puma corporation recognized Dan's talent and wanted him to evaluate Puma corporation's complete benefits package for the purpose of making needed changes without the help of costly outside consultants and Frances believed that Puma's benefits package was outdated and needed to be revised. However, Frances felt Dan disliked to discuss with her to evaluate the total benefits package from her several encouraging because Dan seemed to be constantly thinking of and discussing his outdoor activities and he seemed lack of commitment to do his job. As ERG theory indicated that a person's existence needs don't necessarily have to be satisfied before who can became concerned about whose relationships with others or about using whose personal capabilities, whose desire to meet the existence needs may be stronger than whose desire to meet the two other types of needs, such as relationship with others or about using those personal capabilities, but the other needs may still be important. As this case, Dan , this company 's benefits administrator who chose to serve this company, instead of salary was paid well reason, the other reason was his job was located to let him to enjoy the outdoors sport activities conveniently. Hence, it is Dan's existence needs in this company. Hence, even Frances , this company compensation director accepted to increase Dan's salary to promote him to do higher rank after six months, due to Dan's personal capabilities was very good. Dan whose behaviour performance disliked to discuss with Frances to evaluate and Dan seemed to be constantly thinking of and discussing his outdoor activities and he seemed lack of commitment to his job. As ERG theory indicated Dan could not motivated by Frances because Frances needed him to forgive to enjoy his outdoor sport entertainment when Frances needed him to spend much time to discuss with her to evaluate the total benefits package at this moment. However, Dan felt the reason of his existence was staying in this company was because his new job could located in Utah to always enjoyed the outdoor entertainment. If he could not spend extra time to enjoy this kind of entertainment. It would cause Dan lost commitment to serve this employer.

● suggestion of performance managment strategy raise financial service salespeople sale effort

Using ERG theory, explain the reasons for the situation described in the case.

ERG theory suggests people are motivated by three hierarchically ordered types of needs: existence needs (E), relatedness needs (R) and growth needs (G). A person may work at the same time, although satisfying lower order needs often takes place before a person is strongly motivated by higher level needs.Work motivation and job satisfaction means the relationship between the organization and its members is influenced by what motivates them to work and the rewards and fulfilment they derive from it. Motivation is typified as an individual phenomenon. Every person is unique and all the major theories of motivation allow for this uniqueness to be demonstrated in one way or another, it is as intentional to assume to be under the worker's control and behaviours that are influenced by motivation, such as effort expended. Motivation is through an understanding of internal cognitive processes, that is what people feel and how who think. This understanding should help the manager to predict likely behaviour of staff in given situations. The two factors of greatest importance are what gets people activated and the force of an individual to engage in desired behaviour (direction or choice of behaviour). The purpose of motivation theories is predict behaviour. Motivation isn't the behaviour itself and it is not performance. Motivation concerns action and the internal and external forces which influence a person's choice of action.

Maslow's hierarchy of needs theory suggests people are motivated by their desire to satisfy specific needs and that needs are arranged in a hierarchy with physiological needs at the bottom and self actualization needs at the top. People most satisfy needs at lower levels before being motivated by needs at higher levels. However, ERG theory differs from Maslow's theory. Firstly, a person's existence needs don't necessarily have to be satisfied before who can become concerned about whose relationships with others or about using whose personal capabilities, whose desire to meet the existence needs may be stronger than whose desire to meet the two other types of needs, such as relationship with others or about using those personal capabilities, but the other needs may still be important. Otherwise, the need hierarchy theory proposes that the hierarchy is fixed and that physiological needs must be largely satisfied before other needs become important. Hence, using ERG theory to apply to this case, it may explain why Don Coggin did these behaviour. Although, Frances Mead , compensation director for Puma corporation , who paid well to hire Don Coggin to fill position of benefits administrator for her company in corporate personnel department at Puma, headquartered in Salt Lake city, Utah and the job was located in Utah. Hence, Don could always enjoyed the outdoor and he liked to backpack, camp and did some mountain climbing sport entertainment conveniently. Hence, it ensured that this job location could give Dan to enjoy his likely mountain climbing ,camp, backpack sport entertainment conveniently was also an important reason to influence Don to choose this job.In fact, Dan's financial background aided him greatly in his new benefits administrator job, where he was responsible for development and administration of the pension plan, life and health insurance package, employee stock purchase plan and other employee benefit programs within one month. Dan has learned how to do duties. Frances Mead, she was satisfied with her selection for Dan to do this benefits administrator position. Hence, she expected Dan to move up to in the department rank rapidly, but Dan only concern was that who did not seem to have enough time to enjoy his outdoor activities after he had seem promoted to do further duties absolutely. It implied that Dan disliked to promote to spend more time to do more job duties.

Even, his salary would not be increased and his rank would be promoted in this moment. After six months, Dan had his job proficiently and who was quite talented and the job did not present a strong challenge to him. During to Frances, compensation director for Puma corporation recognized Dan's talent and wanted him to evaluate Puma corporation's complete benefits package for the purpose of making needed changes without the help of costly outside consultants and Frances believed that Puma's benefits package was outdated and needed to be revised. However, Frances felt Dan disliked to discuss with her to evaluate the total benefits package from her several encouraging because Dan seemed to be constantly thinking of and discussing his outdoor activities and he seemed lack of commitment to do his job. As ERG theory indicated that a person's existence needs don't necessarily have to be satisfied before who can became concerned about whose relationships with others or about using whose personal capabilities, whose desire to meet the existence needs may be stronger than whose desire to meet the two other types of needs, such as relationship with others or about using those personal capabilities, but the other needs may still be important. As this case, Dan , this company 's benefits administrator who chose to serve this company, instead of salary was paid well reason, the other reason was his job was located to let him to enjoy the outdoors sport activities conveniently. Hence, it is Dan's existence needs in this company. Hence, even Frances , this company compensation director accepted to increase Dan's salary to promote him to do higher rank after six months, due to Dan's personal capabilities was very good. Dan whose behaviour performance disliked to discuss with Frances to evaluate and Dan seemed to be constantly thinking of and discussing his outdoor activities and he seemed lack of commitment to his job. As ERG theory indicated Dan could not motivated by Frances because Frances needed him to forgive to enjoy his outdoor sport entertainment when Frances needed him to spend much time to discuss with her to evaluate the total benefits package at this moment.

However, Dan felt the reason of his existence was staying in this company was because his new job could located in Utah to always enjoyed the outdoor entertainment. If he could not spend extra time to enjoy this kind of entertainment. It would cause Dan lost commitment to serve this employer. Hence, as ERG theory indicated that Dan felt he and Frances relationship would become worse and he would feel this company was not to be valued for whom to grow further and Dan would plan to leave current employer possibly if Frances continue to force Dan to discuss with her to evaluate the total benefits package for her employer. Moreover, ERG theory also indicated that when a need is satisfied, it may remain the dominant motivator if the next need in the hierarchy can't be satisfied. As Dan , benefits administrator who had satisfied whose relatedness needs to Frances, as Frances had believed who was satisfied with her selection to do this benefits administrator position absolutely within this six months.

Basically, Dan felt his existence needs was satisfied with Frances, compensation director relationship. Hence, during Dan was stilling doing this benefits administration position within these six months, it might remain Dan to be this company dominant motivator, even, he could not promote to do higher rank and he could earn higher salary from Frances after these six months. In result, Dan's performance began to be poor after six months, e.g. complaints from employees regard errors and time delays in insurance claims and stock purchases began to increase. Also, Dan was package and thus no progress in the design of new benefit programs and he began to call in sick occasionally. Interestingly, he seemed to be sick on Friday and Monday, allowing for a three day weekend. It was obvious that

Dan had the ability to perform the job and even more challenging tasks. In conclusion, Dan changed his behaviour and performance poorly in this company because Dan felt not he had existence needs, as he needed to spend time to discuss with Frances to evaluate the total benefits package employees, she could not let him to have more extra time to enjoy his sport entertainment as well as Dan, benefits administrator and Frances, compensation director both co-operation relationship was broken because the reason of Frances needed Dan to spend much time to discuss with her to evaluate Puma corporation's completion benefits package for the purpose of making needed changes was that she did not without the help of costly outside consultants and Frances was still not ensuring to increase his salary, she was examining Dan's ability in this stage. Hence, Frances's decision would cause Dan lost existence needs and relatedness needs and growth needs in this company. Due to these needs had been found to decrease to Dan as they were not satisfied and the lesser needs were not satisfied and the lesser are desired . Hence, it would cause Dan's behaviour and performance to be poor because Frances could not motivate Dan to get these psychological needs absolutely in this company after six months.

Using expectancy theory, explain the reasons for the time pressure reducing feeling situation to the finance service team.

Expectancy theory suggests motivation is a function of an individuals expectancy that a given amount of effort will lead to particular level of performance and judgement that indicates performance will lead to certain outcomes. Expectancy is the subjective probability that a given amount of effort will lead to a particular level of performance. Hence, manager needs to consider the factor of probability that a given amount of effort will lead to a particular level of performance and the second factor individuals consider is the perceived connection between a particular level of performance and important outcomes and the third factor is the importance of each anticipated outcome.Hence, it means individual may have different goals or needs and individual may have different connections between actions and achievement of goals to consider alternatives, weigh cost and benefit and choose action of maximum utility. Different reward can be given to individual as a result of effort or performance. Hence, expectancy theory indicates that people are influences by the expected results of their actions.

Concept of motivation is some driving force within individuals by which they attempt to achieve some goal in order to fulfil some need or expectation. People's behaviours are determined by what motivates them.Their performance is a product of both ability level and motivation. Motivation is a function of the relationship between effort expended and perceived level of performance and the expectation that rewards (desired outcomes) will be related to performance and the expectation that rewards (desired outcomes) are available. Motivation includes extrinsic and intrinsic two kind of motivations. Extrinsic motivation is related to tangible rewards such as salary and benefits, security, promotion, contract of service, the work environment and conditions of work as well as intrinsic motivation is related to psychological rewards, such as the opportunity to use one's ability, a sense of challenge and achievement, receiving appreciation, positive recognition and being treated in a caring and considerate manner.People are capable and willing to perceive fairness in their immediate environment, compare input , ability, skill, age, education, effort and training to outcome like monetary reward, praise, status, improved promotion opportunities to compare reward to others. It implies needs and expectations of staffs at work, it includes economic rewards, social relationships, intrinsic satisfaction. Hence, motivation is as psychological forces that determine the direction of a person's behaviour in an organization and a person's level of effort and a person's level of persistence. It is important that managers attempt to reduce potential frustration, for example, through, effective

recruitment, selection and socialisation, training and development, job design and work organization, equitable human resource management policies, recognition and reward, effective communications,participative styles of management, attempting to understand the individual's perception of the situation. Proper attention to motivation and to the needs and expectation of people at work will help overcome boredom and frustration induced behaviour.

To apply this expectancy theory to this case study. In fact, Dan who had lack effort and motivation to do this benefits administrator position from Frances after six months, so Dan should choose to perform whose normal job duties poorly. e.g. complaints from employees regarding errors and time delays in insurance claims and stock purchases began to increase. Even, Dan was making no progress in the evaluation of benefit package and thus no progress in the design of new benefit programs and he began to call in sick occasionally. Interestingly, he seemed to be sick on Friday and Monday, allowing for a three day weekend. It was obvious that Dan had the ability to perform the job and even more challenging tasks.The expectancy theory could explain reasons why Dan's behaviour and performance was became poor. Due to expectancy theory suggests motivation is a function of an individual's expectancy that a given amount of effort will lead a particular level of performance and judgement that indicates performance will lead to certain outcomes. Before the six months, Frances could give motivation to Dan, such as she could give good salary and good job location to satisfy Dan's life needs and outdoor sport entertainment needs and Dan and Frances both felt this job's working hours and Dan's ability and performance was very reasonable.

However, after six months, Frances needed Dan to spend much time to discuss with her to evaluate the total benefits package for her employees, but Frances could not tell Dan to ensure to increase Dan's salary and promotion after Dan should finish this extra evaluation job duties with Frances. Even, Dan felt who could not enjoy this outdoor sport entertainment due to he needed to spend much time to discuss with Frances about the total benefits package evaluation to whose employees issue. Hence,Dan would felt that who spent much effort to do this job, but he could not get fair salary and position . It would cause him to decide to change his job performance and personal behaviour to be poor , e.g. complaints from employees regarding, errors and time delays in insurance claims and stock purchases began to increase. Even, Dan was also making no progress in the evaluation of benefit package and this no progress in the design of new benefit programs and he began to call in sick occasionally. Interestingly, he seemed to be sick on Friday and Monday, allowing for a three day weekend. It was obvious that Dan had the ability (effort) to perform to job (benefit administrator position) in this Puma corporation company, but he chose to perform to do this position poorly. The reason was because Dan had judged that his expectancy was not reasonable from Frances demand because Dan needed to spend much time to discuss with Frances and who could not get higher salary and higher rank and who could not have extra time to enjoy his outdoor entertainment. Hence, Dan's decision to make poor performance and bad behaviour, his aim was to make Frances felt who had ability to change another new job possibly. Unless, Frances could change her decision not needed Dan to spend much time to discuss with her to deal this extra job duties. Otherwise, who would find another new job possibly. It implied Dan's job expectancy was not same to Frances's performance need expectancy to Dan to cause Dan's poor performance occurred after six month.

Using the integration framework found in the last major section of the chapter, describe what actions Frances should and should not take if Frances expects his finance service sales team can feel less time pressure to sell their finance service packages to their customers in short time easily.

In fact, Dan Coggin, benefits administrator, whose behaviour performance indicated that who chose to do this job because he felt be well paid and this job was located in Utah to always enjoy the outdoors activities of backpack, camp and do some mountain climbing. Before six months, Dan's job performance was satisfied with Frances, compensation director, so it caused Dan expected Dan to move up in the department ranks rapidly . Due to Frances felt Puma's benefits package was outdated and needed to revised and who proposed to making needed changes, without the help of costly outside consultants. Thus, Frances decided to recognize Dan's talents and wanted him spent extra time to evaluate with her to discuss how Puma corporation's complete benefits package to make changed to satisfy Puma's employees benefits of needs. However, after six months, Dan's performance and behaviour began to be poor, e.g. complaints from employees regarding errors and time delays in insurance claims and stock purchase began to increase. Also, Dan was making no progress in the evaluation of benefit package and thus no

progress in the design of new benefit programs and he began to call in sick occasionally. Interestingly, he seemed to be sick on Friday and Monday, allowing for a three day weekend. It was obvious that Dan had the ability to perform the job and even more challenging tasks.

However, why Dan became lazy and who disliked to spend extra time to discuss with Frances to evaluate how to change Puma corporation's complete benefits package to its employees. It was obvious that Frances forced Dan to spend extra time to discuss with her to do evaluation issue that who did not enquire Dan's desire(ideas) whether who liked or disliked to do this issue and Dan would feel who would not have time to enjoy his sport activities in this job Utah location and who also felt it was unfair to him why whose salary was not increased and position was not promoted when Dan needed to spend extra time to do extra job unreasonably.

I shall use integration framework to find whether what Frances Mead, compensation director should take actions and should not take actions if he expects to achieve time pressure reducing feeling to his finance service sale teams . On the one hand, Frances should take these actions as below:

In common, formulating strategies that can deliver competitive advantage is not easy. Senior managers needed to work with other individuals engage in meetings, experiments, discussion and analyses in order to create or modify company strategies. Implementing strategies and engaging in the day-to-day behaviours that help to create competitive advantage also are not easy task. Hence, staffs must be motivated if who are to effectively engage in the behaviours and practices that bring advantage and success to a firm. Hence, Frances mead, compensation director should need to choose to use different strategies to require different types of people (staffs) and behaviours and therefore different approaches to motivation.

To fully motivate such Dan, benefits administrator staff, resource for trying new ideas, must be available, including time and opportunities to develop new skills to change old pension plan, life and health insurance package, employee stock purchase plan and other employee benefit programs benefit package. I believe human resources and time was not enough to Frances and Dan two people to evaluate this issue. Frances ought to enquire Dan's idea whether Dan felt what cause whose performance began to be poor, e.g. complaints from employee regarding errors and time delays in insurance claims and stock purchase began to increase. To investigate whether Dan felt the issue of evaluation Puma corporation's complete benefits package issue with her or other factors that was influenced to his normal job performance to be poor. The benefits were that Frances could let Dan to tell what the reasons were to cause his performance poor honestly and their conservation could let Dan felt France could spend extra time to consider to discuss whether what Dan felt needs and dissatisfaction to cause Dan's performance poorly. Hence, Frances could judge whether Dan's ability could deal to evaluate Puma corporation's complete benefits package and this issues could not influence Dan's daily normal job duties for this benefits administrator position or not. If Frances should prefer to spend extra time to discuss with Dan about what difficulty and needs and dissatisfaction who felt to cause whose job performance began to be poor. Frances should know whether it was job factors or other factors were influenced to Dan to feel dissatisfaction to cause whose performance poorly to let Frances to revise whose strategies. The factors could include such as, unreasonable market salary, poor working environment, increasing job responsibilities and feeling difficulties, lacking opportunity for advancement or promotion, challenging work and potential for personal growth, lacking personal commitment and recognition and achievement needs to this position,lacking work and life balance needs, unreasonable company policies and working conditions and administration procedures, poor interpersonal relationship with peer and poor status security issues.

As goal setting theory suggests challenging and specific goals increase human performance because whose effort and persistence attention can be committed to affect motivation. Due to Frances didn't indicate clear specific goals to let Dan to know whether how and what steps who should use to evaluate Dan's ability to judge whose job performance was achieved to goal to promote higher rank before Dan began to do this job. Hence, Dan should feel doubt why Frances needed him to spend extra time to evaluate with Frances about making changes to Puma corporation's complete benefits package issue after six months. Hence, Frances should need to explain why who needed Dan to spend extra time to evaluate with him and they also needed to discuss further issue for this evaluation report job of about how difficult Dan felt his performance goal should be achieved whether the goal should be easy, moderately difficult or very difficult to achieve to Dan's ability, how the expert outcome should be specific or goals could be more do best what Dan needed to make commitment to achieve this goal; to what extent of feedback needs Dan should be informed of their report in this evaluation progress toward his performance goal. Hence, if Frances could let Dan to know what Dan needed to perform to achieve. Frances goal to evaluate Dan's ability clearly. Then, Dan's could judge whether Frances was a right employer for his continue staying or leaving further decision. An understanding for the factors that motivate workers are critical not only to corporate executive who concentrate on the bottom line, but more importantly to the security of companies as it relates to compete in the global market.

However, the internal process view that motivation needs that activate, guide, and motivate behaviour (especially goal directed behaviour) is one of the most important concerns of modern organizational managers , as Frances Mead, compensation director for Puma corporation. The traditional motivator for a worker is his salary, but in many cases that isn't enough. As Puma corporation, Frances Mead, compensation director, it implied to use only material rewards to motivate Dan, benefits administrator staff , it was not enough and it needed to use only motivators to satisfy Dan's needs. Supposing to Dan's tasks such as development and administration of pension plan, life and health insurance and employee stock purchase package etc duties whose solution was obvious extrinsic motivators, e.g. increasing salary reward were working as which should be increase performance, but for task whose solution were more complex, such as revision and evaluation of complete outdated benefits package for the purpose how to make needed changes, extrinsic motivation should have negative effects on performance to Dan. Hence, if the task was complex, the motivation users must be intrinsic e.g. achievement, chance, promotion to give to Dan employee. Due to revision and evaluation of complete outdated benefits package was one complex and if also needed to spend more resources and time discussion tasks for Puma corporation. Hence, Frances should ought to tell Dan who should use job with performance related pay to attract him of higher ability and induced who to provide greater effort. Frances should focuses on Dan's role as an incentive system. Hence, Frances should consider compensation as a return for Dan's services rendered and saw Dan's performance was as a reflection of whose personal worth in terms of skills and abilities as well as whose education and training also had acquired. However, Frances should view compensation from two perspectives: as a major expense and as a possible influence on Dan's attitudes and behaviours through compensation based motivational strategies. This potential to influence Dan's work attitudes and behaviours and subsequently the productivity and effectiveness of Puma corporation.

Attribute theory indicated that when an outcome, such as poor performance is attributed to a stable cause. such as low intelligence, it is logical to expect that the employee's performance isn't going to change in the future. If the same poor performance is attributed to a less stable factor, such as insufficient effort, a employer can expect that the employee could improve whose performance by working harder in the future. Thus, Frances should consider what attributions were to influence Dan's job performance began to be poor, then who should revise whose actions should be changed to solve this issue. The attribution should influence Dan's performance to be poor, internal and stable attribution, such as whether Dan's intelligence could deal his normal job duties and extra job duties of evaluation on Puma's benefits package both at the same time; external and unstable attribution, such as whether Dan had enough effort and time to attempt to discuss with Frances to finish this extra job duties of
evaluation on Puma's benefits package within limited time or external and unstable attribution, such as whether Frances' temporary strategy or

decision was without the help of outside consultants to evaluate Puma's benefits package whether which should give pressure or effort to Dan to attempt to help him to finish this evaluation job, it meant that Dan would do this duties, even which should also influence whose normal duties to be poor if Dan felt pressure to attempt to do this extra duties. Frances should need to provide feedback to Dan about whose progress toward performance goals was well established . In fact, feedback on performance was likely to have a positive effect on motivation. Moreover, Dan's feedback was important when benefits package of evaluation of performance goals existed and when Dan was relatively difficult to achieve. Hence, Frances's feedback should encourage Dan to discover (find) errors to know what he should need to improve during evaluation was progressing and Frances should not have due date limitation to let Dan felt pressure to finish this benefit plan evaluation job ,even if influenced to whose normal job duties poorly .

Expectancy theory provides a useful framework for organizing those factors : people will be committed to goals that carrying a reasonable expectation of being attained and are more viewed as desirable to attain. Frances should judge whether human resource inputs were enough to do this benefit package evaluation job with Dan. It was possible that Dan felt human resource inputs were out enough to cause who felt pressure to attempt to dot this extra job duties with Frances and Dan should feel inequity and unfair treatment and unreasonable due to who should need to spend extra time to do this extra evaluation job with Frances. Hence, Frances should need to explain to let Dan to know why who needed Dan to attempt to do this extra evaluation job as well as what benefits were Dan should give reward if Dan's evaluation job performance could satisfy Frances' requirement. Then Dan would be committed to goals that carrying a reasonable expectation of being attained and was more viewed as desirable to attain. On the other hand, Frances should not take these actions as below: Although Dan performance began to become poor after six months due to Dan needed to spend extra time to discuss with Frances to evaluate how to change Puma corporation old benefits package issue. However, Frances should not angry to blame Dan immediately. The reason was that Dan's performance was still good before six months. It meant that who had ability to do this position.Hence, Dan ought have ability to assist Frances to evaluate the changed needs to current benefits package evaluation to Puma corporation's employees with Frances discussion together.

Otherwise, if Frances should blame to Dan. it would cause Dan felt Frances was not a good compensation director to manage and co-operate with him to work together and it was possible that would choose to leave Puma corporation to find any employer immediately. Then, Frances would feel difficult to spend more time to choose applicants to re-employ another new staff to do this benefit administrator position, instead of Dan and Frances should also need to spend more time to train this new staff. Hence, Frances should not blame Dan. Otherwise, Frances should need to enquire why Dan's performance to be poor whether Dan's poor performance behaviour was caused by extra evaluation job duties factor or other personal factors to revise Dan's errors to expect Dan to continue to assist Frances to finish this evaluation job effectively and efficiently.

In conclusion, I did not agree Frances, compensation director should blame Dan immediately because Dan believed himself had owned market competitive ability due to Dan had worked in Puma corporation six months . It should give Dan had confidence to change another new employer if Dan felt Frances' personal attitude was not friendly to arrange any further new jobs to him to do. Hence, Frances should enquire Dan why who performed poorly in order to solve whose personal trouble issues and then Frances should also attempt to find some methods to satisfy Dan's personal needs to motivate and persuade Dan to continue to co-operate with Frances in this company together.

CHAPTER SIX

Employee Engagement Strategy

Employee engagement aim

What is employee engagement? The term employee engagement needs to be clearly understood by every organization. Some organizations perceive it as job satisfaction others say it's the emotional attachment towards the organization. Employee Engagement is a fundamental concept in the effort to understand and describe, both qualitatively and quantitatively, the nature of the relationship between an organization and its employees. An "engaged employee" is defined as one who is fully absorbed by and enthusiastic about their work and takes positive action to further the organization's reputation and interests. An engaged employee has a positive attitude towards the organization and its values.

An organization with "high" employee engagement might therefore be expected to outperform those with "low" employee engagement. Employee engagement improves the productivity of an organization as the practice helps the employees in teamwork, co-ordination and inter-personal skills. It means that such as morale and job satisfaction. Despite academic critiques, employee-engagement practices are well established in the management of human resources and of internal communications. Employee engagement today has become synonymous with terms like 'employee experience' and 'employee satisfaction'. The relevance is much more due to the vast majority of new generation professionals in the workforce who have a higher propensity to be 'distracted' and 'disengaged' at work.

The workplace environment impacts employee morale, productivity and engagement - both positively and

negatively. The work place environment in a majority of industry is unsafe and unhealthy. These includes poorly designed workstations, unsuitable

furniture, lack of ventilation, inappropriate lighting, excessive
noise, insufficient safety measures in fire emergencies and lack of personal protective equipment. People working in such environment are prone to occupational disease and it impacts on employee's performance. Thus productivity is decreased due to the workplace environment. It is the quality of the
employee's workplace environment that most impacts on their level of motivation and subsequent performance. How well they engage with the organization, especially with their immediate environment, influences to a great extent their error rate, level of innovation and collaboration with other employees,
absenteeism and ultimately, how long they stay in the job. Creating a work environment in which employees are productive is essential to increased profits for your organization, corporation or small business. The relationship between work, the workplace and the tools of work, workplace becomes an integral part of work itself. The management that dictate how, exactly, to maximize employee productivity center around two major areas of focus: personal motivation and the infrastructure of the work environment.

In today's competitive business environment, organizations can no longer afford to waste the potential of their workforce. There are key factors in the employee's workplace environment that impact greatly on
their level of motivation and performance. The workplace environment that is set in place impacts employee morale, productivity and engagement - both positively and negatively. It is not just coincidence that new programs addressing lifestyle changes, work/life balance, health and fitness - previously not considered key benefits - are now primary considerations of potential employees, and common practices among the most admired companies.

In an effort to motivate workers, firms have implemented a number of practices such as performance based pay, employment security agreements, practices to help balance work and family, as well as various forms of information sharing. In addition to motivation, workers need the skills and ability to do
their job effectively. And for many firms, training the worker has become a necessary input into the production process.

THE PROBLEM STATEMENT

The work place environment in a majority of industry is unsafe and unhealthy. These includes poorly designed workstations, unsuitable furniture, lack of ventilation, inappropriate lighting, excessive noise, insufficient safety measures in fire emergencies and lack of personal protective equipment. People working in such environment are prone to occupational disease and it impacts on employee's performance. Thus productivity is decreased due to the workplace environment. It is a wide industrial area where the employees are facing a serious problem in their work place like environmental and physical factors. So it is difficult to provide facilities to increase their performance level. Thus, effective employee engagement strategy can assist the organization's employees feel they are the organization's important members to serve their organizations to work more hardly in order to raise productivities easily.

- What is employee welfare mean?

Employee welfare includes everything, such as facilities, benefits and services, that an employer provides or does to ensure comfort of the employees. Good welfare helps to motivate employees and ensure increased productivity.

Providing good welfare to employees may be a costly decision, but the long-term benefits are immense. It is one way of complying with the law, thus ensuring that an employer avoids legal issues. It allows accompany to retain its good and skilled employees for long periods of time. Employees work well in workplaces where they are treated well and respected. Good welfare also helps to create a good company image for a particular employer.

Employee welfare facilities in the organization affects on the behavior the employees as well as on the productivity of the organization. While getting work done through employees the management must provide required good facilities to all employees.

The management should provide required good facilities to all employees in such way that employees become satisfied and they work harder and more efficiently and more effectively.

Welfare is a broad concept referring to a state of living of an individual or a group, in a desirable relationship with the total environment – ecological economic and social. It aims at social development by such means as social legislation, social reform social service, social work, social action. The object of economics welfare is to promote economic production and productivity and through development by increasing equitable distribution. Labour welfare is an area of social welfare conceptually and operationally.

It covers a broad field and connotes a state of well being, happiness, satisfaction, conservation and development of human resources

Employee welfare is an area of social welfare conceptually and operationally. It covers a broad field and connotes a state of well being, happiness, satisfaction, conservation and development of

human resources and also helps to motivation of employee. The basic propose of employee welfare is to enrich the life of

employees and to keep them happy and conducted. Welfare measures may be both Statutory and Non statutory laws require the employer to extend certain benefits to employees in addition to wages or salaries.

Labour Welfare Measures

Labor welfare includes various facilities, services and amenities provided to workers for improving their health,

economic betterment and social status.

Welfare measures are in addition to regular wages and other economic benefits available to workers due to legal

and collective bargaining. The purpose of labor welfare is to bring about the development

of the whole personality of the workers to make a better workforce. The very logic behind providing welfare schemes is to create efficient, healthy, loyal and satisfied labor force for the organization. The purpose of providing such facilities is to make their work life better and also to raise their standard of living.

● Measurement the level of employee engagement factor

There are a number of external and internal factors that help measure the level of employee engagement. External factors include organization environment; its culture and values, manager-subordinate relationship, relationships with co-workers, monetary benefits and appraisals. Whereas internal factors include the personal values of employee, personality type and commitment to work. Gallup's research on employee engagement shows that there is a strong relationship between well being of an employee and the level of their engagement. An engaged employee is efficient an effective for the organizational outcomes.

Employee engagement has direct effect on productivity and growth. If employees are engaged they will try level best to fulfill their job responsibilities which will consequently lead to not only increase in organization productivity but will also enhance the self performance of employee. In the world of globalization only those organizations which have highly engaged workers can survive and grow. But an organization can engage its employees only if the employees have the desired attitude. Therefore an organization should train its employees to change their attitudes if they want to properly manage workforce engagement.

● employee engagement survey reasons

Nowadays, increasing diverse and geographically workforces bring global competition to live nd retain qualified employees aim. Organizations need to attract, motivately and engage employees though not only the core HR functions of compensation, benefits, performance management and talent development, but engagement programs, such as work life effectiveness, recognition and reward systems.

In fact, one strategic employee engagement if designed correctly, is cost-effective program and valuable tools that can measured and increase employee involvement and ethusiasm in their work and contributions to their employer's goals or values. Industry research analysts indicated that companies in the top employee engagement designed program, which can brough 16% higher profits and 18% higher productivity in general. They also evaluated the relationship between employee engagement and employee turnover. Companies with light effective recognition engagement programs have 31 % lower ineffective turnover than organizations with ineffective recognition programs. However, to be most impactful engagement solutions require innovative features to enble full service, effective management of strategic engagement programs. Social communicative elements along with rich analytics and mobile capabilities that interoperate with existing HR solutions are necessary to keep more efficient and effective changing HR needs and organizational goals.

As the economy slowly makes its way back in recovery mode and more employees are concerned with issues beyond job security. So organizations need to concern how to a focus on employee engagement and the criticial factor ithin organizations that drives performance. HR conulting forms point out a relationship between high levels of engagement and high levels of financial performance. Achieving overall employee engagement is overview to have need. For years, companies around the globle have conducted employee engagement surveys in an effort to determine why their organizations function the way they do, and how they can pull organizations to improve performance. The results of there employee engagement surveys sometimes reflect, better and accurate key business decisions and impacting the day-for-day lives of employees, shareholders and customers.

But is that really all these is to real reflection? Should company focus on employee engagement as the key indicator of success or failure within their organization? Is high employee engagement brings some sort of better management skills? It is absolute no answer. When employee engagement should be measured as an important organizations human resource and social system, truly understanding how to optimize performance in your organization requires understanding your organization requires understanding your culture. For example, we know that with some people, we can increase their engagement and satisfaction by simply, making their work easy-opertating in a go along to get along manner and more generally encouraging passive behaviors.

Employee engagement becomes a popular topic of the workplace instead of job satisfaction and organizational commitment which is approved to effect the organizational outcome. In HR department behaviors that affect th structured interviews were conducted in corporate HR to explore the employee engagement and techniques for improving employee engagement were recommended based on the interview.

The quantitative research results show that job autonomy , performance feedback, challenging work, worker person fit, development support and the connection with co-workers have a strong relationship with employee engagement. And the recommended solutions like building on action team, have more team activities and develop a formal both for big team (corporate HR) and smaller team will improve their engagement over time. Organizations need to increase their performance by both efficiency and productivity. Managers would hardly deny that employees make a criticial difference in innovation, organization performance, competitiveness and lead to the business success. Hence, HR plays an important role in the employee engagement program with the responsibilities of the survey, providing feedback on results, prommoting communication in different groups of people, encouraging people to take action and providing educational opportunities. Employees growth, teamwork mangement support and basic needs are needed to measure by relevant questions in viewpoint survey by using five point scale. Personal growth is measured by talking about the progress and having job opportunity grow. The options count, mission and purpose fellow employees who committed to quality work and having a best friend at work and identified as the questions for measuring team work . Management support is measured by opportunity to do the best , recognition or praise care and encourage the development.

Employee survey can reflect employees engagement , e.g. one viewpoint survey for the past three years and every time survey has chance to let employees fill the survey in, then HR managers can get the results to give scores. Managers should take get move real feedback from different department staff's positive or negative emotion or feeling aboug whose job tasks, whether they worry about any job difficulties. Hence, surveys can let organizations try to figure out of their employees are engaged and how to make them engaged by using different surveys and tools to stay competitive and improve performance.

In survey contents, there are four main topics in the engagement survey: growth, teamwork, managment support and basic needs. The result can show the most items in engagement support were scored relatively low or high as mean of development support from manager. Hence, many organizations were focusing on designing a successful reward system to keep employees engaged and productive line or the low level managers who can serve their employees are typically the ones who work or fail the engagement tools because line managers need often communicate and contact workers when they are working. They can know what their feeling to their job tasks whether it is positive or negative emotion in order to find solutions how to raise their performance.

● How to build talent staffing source

Marion, D. & Michel, S. (2014) explained talent is the sum of a person's abilities, his or her intrinsic grifts, skills, knowledge, experience, intelligence, judgement, attitude, character and drive. It also includes his or her ability to learn. At the international level, talent shortages are more severe. During the past decade, an internationally mobile group of employees, who can pick and choose where they work. As firms in employing markets also begin competing in the global economy, these people are in ever-greater demand. For example, Singapore has had on an intensive recruitment program for skilled foreign workers, with more liberal criteria for eligibility to work in the country. Some 90,000 now work in the city-state, the majority from the US, UK, France, Australia, Japan and South Korea.

Marion, D. & Michel, S. (2014) indicated several factors need to be taken into account to understand the market for skilled labour. Hays and Oxford

Economics pooled their data to identify seven components that together give a better picture of skill shortages as below:

Labour-market participation means the degree to which a country's talent pool is fully utilized, for example, whether women and older workers have access to jobs; labour -market flexibility means the legal and regulatory environment is faced by business, especially how easily immigrants can fill talent gaps; wage pressure overall means whether real wages are keeping pace with inflation; wage pressure in high-skill industries means which wages in high-skill industries outpace those in low-skill industries; wage pressure in high-skill occupations means rises in wages for highly skilled workers are a short -term indicaton of skills shortages, talent mismatches means the mismatch between the skills are needed by businesses and those available, are indicated by the number of long-term unemployed and job vacancies; educational flexibility means whether the educational system can adapt to meet the future needs of organizations for talent, especially in the fields of mathematics and science.

Firms operating in knowledge-intensive industries depend on their most capable staff to help create value through intangible assets, such as patents, licence and technical know-how. In fact, globalisation and technological competition brings to much complexity of many jobs and occupations. Firms are now looking for individuals with an range of abilities that might include specialized skills, broader functional skills, industry expertise and knowledge of specific geographical markets. The skills include: digital skill means the fast growing digital economy is increasing the demand for highly skilled technical workers. Companies are looking for staff with social-media based skills, especially in " digital expression". Agile thinking means the regulatory and environment uncertainty, such as life sciences and energy and mining industry's talent knowledge, ability skill is needed for employee's personal effort and characteristic needs; interpersonal and communication skill, H R managers predict that co-creativity and brainstorming skills be greatly in demand, it will bring relationship building and teamwork skills; global operating skill means that ability to manage diverse employee is seen as the most important global operating skill,, glocalisation (where home-market products and services are tailored to the taste of overseas customers and innovation (where staffs lead innovation and then the company applies these new ideas to mature markets).

Talent is a relative concept, it includes these components, such as technical specialists, especially in areas key to the organization's core capabilities, individuals with hard-to-recruit skills, bright individuals from underrepresented groups whom the positions , the best-performing graduates or school leavers and managers with the potential to move into senior management positions at the local, national or international level. However, judgement effort is the main factor to influence organizations to select individuals whose behavior and values fit with those of the organization. How performance and potential are measured is for senior managers to decide.

In many cases, the definition of exceptional performance is explained in competency frameworks and appraisal systems. Defining high potential can be more difficult and might include a range of assessment tools, such as development centers, psychometric testing and the personal judgement of those whose insights into talent are widely respected.

Talent plan has three components: talent gaps mean HR works with business management levels. Once a year to identify which leadership , management and functional skills are needed, how those roles and responsibilities and whether the talent processes are producing people who will be able to solve these skill gaps; talent supply means most of the focus is on management trainees and a smaller proportion of people who are recruited mid-career; talent development means recruiting high-potential individuals at the start of their careers and taking them through a structured development program.

Talent strategy means how senior leaders can identify the capabilities that help achieve the company's strategy strategic objectives and provide a competitive effort. These capabilities are not just tactical or operational skills, which although important, do have as much of an impact on business performance and profit. Operational management or senior levels and the talent management team then break down each capabilities into parts, such as specific skills, knowledge and expertise. They look at how these skills sets enable each business unit to deliver their part of the strategic plan.

This analysis should indicate the roles where knowledge and expertise are needed for maximum business value. There are not automatically senior leadership or management values. They also extend to technical and specialist roles or to previously overlooked roles, e.g. positions within the organization that help sure that expertise from one part of the business. Part of review many necessitate a fresh look at knowledge management processes across the business. The HR team should also review its own ways of working and thinking o make sure that its processes for recruitment, selection, learning and development, appraisal , reward and recognition and concentrates on the skills, cultural values and behaviors most critical to business performance.

Talent review aims to assess how well employees are performing currently in the critical roles, identified by the strategic review, and their potential to move into more demanding roles. Some of the required data will be held centrally by HR, but almost certainly, the team carrying out the review will need to speak directly to operational and line managers to get feedback about the performance and potential of key individuals.

At part of the review, gap analysis will help identify gaps in skills necessary to carry out the business's strategy and plans and whether any critical roles are unfilled. Succession planning is a important factor here as it may well be that insufficient numbers of potential successors have been identified for certain critical roles. A talent based gap analysis main aim is to focus on hiring and/or training needs as part of a talent strategy, it is the company's strategic planning process. It draws ona wide source of data, both internally and externally. It looks at strategic needs both current and future, and makes judgements about operational needs.

This analysis determines whether the right talented people are in the right position at the right time. These three factors will influence whether talent planning needs to be improved. For example, right people, but wrong time, it means that people who might not be being used currently because of ao downturn in markets, but who the organization does not want to lose as it takes too much time and money to replace them when demand increases. The organization must therefore determine its strategy for retaining and motivating them; wrong people means that people are not employed to perform the work .

This suggests that a mistake is between HR processes and the business strategy, learning and development processes may not be keeped good with changing business needs. There may be needed to appraise and promote to make right decisions that are leading to a mismatch between roles and people, right people, but wrong location. It means that people who can do the work , but are in the wrong location as a result of a reorganization and constraints on mobility, make more creative use of temporary assignments and virtual working, or relocate work to where it can be done by the most skilful employees.

Finally, once the talent review has identified any shortagesof talent, an organization has three options: either buying talent through external recuritment or building talent through tailored learning and development programmes that involve work experiences that will help talent employment development or borrowing talent by resorting to temporary workers or outsourcing.

Buying talent is an obvious choice when a company needs particular skills or expertise that it does not have time or ability ro develop in existing staff is to buy in that talent. The task is then to source this expertise, and offer the right set of inducements to recruit and retain individuals with the desired skills. However, buying talent can be costly as the going rate for sought-after specialists is high and they are often in a strong negotiating position. For example, swift recuritment processes and flexible remuneration package can attract talent employees' applications through external recuritment seeking recritment method.

Borrowing talent is a temporary need for specialist skills it makes sense to borrow or " rent" what is required by contracting with, for example, freelancers, independent consultants, staff on seondment or firms that will supply staff. This form of flexible labour means uncertain times such flexibility becomes more attractive because it enables firms to assemble new combinatins of skills in swift reponse to sudden shifts in their environment. It provides firms with access to wider pool of talent, especially in the case of work that can be performed in any location.

This, building talent means that a larger firm will seek to build its own talent by creating a reliable high potential and high performing employees. The aim is to rise and train talent skilful employees' qualities and efforts and to invest in their careers in the expectation that they will progress to senior positions in the business. So, these individuals are placed in a talent pool where their progress is monitored and where they are given extra opportunities for training and development. To keep talented people to develop, there is an emphasis on performance management, so any weaknesses or developments are needed to find.

● sourcing staff methods

Internal sources advantages of filling a vacancy internally, they include better motivation because employee capabilities are more ensured to promote or transfer, improved moral, performance and loyalty to the employee, lower staff turnover rate, better utilisation of employees because he/she owns more abilities in a different job or capacity , less training required, greater reliability than external recruitment because a present employee is the terms of personality, attitudes, values, work habits etc.

known more, being quicker and cheaper than external recruitment.

External source advantages when the company need to expand and growth contribute to the need for recruitment. Other factors include resignation, dismissal, retirement and relocation. Although internal recruitment has many advantages, many positions are filled by external applicants. When an internal candidate is transferred or promoted, it means that his/her position then because a vacancy, presuming that there is no reduction in staff numbers and no organizational restructuring. Hence, external recruitment can be time consuming , expensive and uncertain. However, organizations still need to conduct the external sources selecting method on a regular basis. The external recruitment source channels may include internal online or newspaper advertising, private employment agencies, professional bodies appointment services, local employment services office of government labor department, direct links with universities, colleges and schools, unsolicited applications, recommendations by present employees or by other employers' referrals.

Talent management steps in validating a test. Test aims to ensure whether the test listening and speaking competence, he/she owns the skillful effort is enough to do the vacancy or position in the organization. The steps in validating a test is as below:

The organization needs to analyze the job. It is necessary to conduct a careful job analysis to produce a good job description and an appropriate job specification. These requirements can then become the objectives of the selection tests. Then, it needs to choose the test from among the various testing means, choose the one that is the most valid and reliable. Next, it needs to administer the test. One can either test current employees and find out of there is any significant differences between the scores and the employees' performances , it means concurrent validation or test potential candidates before they are hired and compare their scores with their performances after they have been in their jobs, it means predictive validation.

However, predictive validation may have disadvantages, e.g. job performance may be difficult to assess objectively, the process of validation may be lengthy, the results of the test are compared with the performance of a selected group only, it is not completely validated. Concurrent validation is quick, but its disadvantages may include standardisation is difficult, the test is validated against a non-typical group only, i.e. present employers rather than candidates for employment, the present employee may not behave normally when they do the test.

Reference
Marion, D. & Michel, S. (2014) the economist, Managing talent, Profile books ltd, London, UK, pp.1-2, 6.

● Engagement strategy solves human resource
international organization
strategic challenges

When one company is one international company, it needs have offices are located in overseas. So, its staffs will be different countries' people and people's cultures are totally different. It will influence how they cooperate to work in teams efficiently together. If they feel difficult communication, then will have possible to bring poor performance or inefficient productivities. So, one firm has office(s) in overseas. The human resource (HR) department needs to consider how to deal to let every different countries' staffs feel easy communication in order to cooperate efficiently. It will increase to need for highly qualified multicultural managers as organizations globalize their operations. Therefore, a resource-based view of human resource management is needed to utilized. In view of human capital needs to provide insight into the value of managers to have unique local market knowledge, i.e. social knowledge. So, they can help organizations to develop / maintain a distinct competitive advantage in the markets they enter, if they hope to enter overseas market to sell their services to the country market successfully.

It brings these question: How will these global population and economic change impact the HR management practices of global organizations in overseas market development? How to maintain resources in various increase competitive advantage against global competitors, when the organization needs to develop overseas market?

I shall indicate case , such as how Japan firms can implement human resource strategy to manage their foreign employees when their organizations hope to enter overseas market? The typically Japanese ways in which Japanese companies have long arranged their human resource strategies are certainly changing.

However, Japan's organizational culture is different to overseas countries, e.g. US, UK etc. western countries' organizational cultures. Hence the Japan company needs to change it's culture to attempt to adapt western countries' staffs cultures, when it plans to set up office(s) in any western (countries). Because it needs to employ western staffs who owned the country's sales experiences to assist its Japanese salepsople to cooperate to sell its poducts to any western country (countries)' market more easily in possible. Alos, it means the Japan firm HR manafers or any department managers need to change whose management attitude to adapt the western countries staffs working culture to cooperate to work in order to achieve to raise performance or improve productive efficiencies.

Hence, the Japan firm's Japanese human resource manager needs to concern how to particular qualify management system to adapt western working culture, consensus decision-making, building foreign employee loyalty to its overseas branch images and avoiding a look of gender equality in the workplace. Japan forms like to train employees, making them to own with a range of skills and abilities that they can contribute to the company throughout their career. Lifetime employment also leads to a decreased turnover rate for company. However, this kind of continue training method, it is not absolute to be adapted to some western countries because some western countries' staffs who do not accept their employers force them often need continue training courses to improve or raise their skills aim. They only like to spend time to attend one time training course finishing or sometime attend in house training courses in their companies. They feel that company is wasting their working time to learn non-essential or unuseful knowledge or skill. So, when a Japan firm needs overseas western staffs need to often be trained, it will bring the western staffs choose to leave its company earlier. So, Japan firm needs to concern continue lifetime training method whether it is suitable to any western countries' staffs to be accepted to spend working time to learn extra new skills or knowledge. For this working suitation example, if one western employee feels busy that he/she needs to finish whose current tasks today immediately, but the company will need he/she attends the training course to learn immediately. Then, it will bring he/she feels worry anout whether he/she can finish his/her tasks today to avoid whose superviser feels angry. Hence, how to arrangement suitable training time , that is imporant factor to influence the western staffs to feel whether the Japan employer really considerate their work need. Hence, Japan human resource management needs to concern how the immediate short -term training course impact will bring western countries employees' complaints and dissatisfaction. Consequently, it is important to influence western employees' performance to be poor of the Japan firm skill needs some countries' western employees often need to attend training courses to learn something immediately.

When one firm needs to set up office(s) to be operated in overseas market. It needs to concern what is the comparative HRM between itself country and foreign countries. For example: Who is living or has lived in a foreign country? Who can speak two or more languages? Who has non-academic work experience? These comparative factors will influence whether the company ought follow what the requirement level to select the most right foreign employees to serve its overseas office organization. Becauuse if the firm can select the most right foreign applicant to do the position in the overseas office(s). It will bring positive long-term consequences: Individual well-being organizational effectiveness and societal well-being. The company needs to considerate the comparative issues, e.g. what is the recruitment and selection difference beteen itself country and its foreign coutries markets when it has no market economy link? What is the working time flexibility need between itself country and its foreign countries markets ? What is the salary level difference between itself country's staffs demand and its foreign countries staffs demand? What is the training need difference between itself country's staffs and ots foreign country staffs' needs? What is the downsizing need difference between itself country and its foreign countries organizations?

Can outsourcing foreign human resource strategy raise foreign employee individual performance? If the company selected to find one foreign job agent to help it to select whom is the right foreign applicant to do the position in overseas office(s). The foreign job agent is located at overseas, such as US office is the China firm's foreign office . So, the foreign job agent company will locate in US. It is better than the firm's home country job agent to outsource staffing selecting job to it to do, because when the outsourcing staff selecting job agent is the firm's home town , but it needs to help the firm to select foreign employees. It is very difficult for it to contact these any foreign applicants as well as the home country's outsoucing selecting foreign employees job agent does not have same working cultural management to know how to help the home country firm to seek the suitable foreign applicants to do any positions to work in its overseas offices more easier than one foreign outsourcing foreign employees selecting job agent.

Hence, it seems that one international organization needs to set up offices to let its different department managers to cooperate with the foreign countries (country) employees. The foreign outsourcing staffing selecting job agent can help it to select the most right foreign applicants to cooperate with the company's local manager(s) more easily. When the organization nees to employ 100 foreign employees, even 100 foreign employees, It's HR department has no enough time to select whom are the most suitable foreign employees to fill the foreign vacancies. Hence, the foreign outsoucing staffing selecting job agent will be the best choice to replace the international firm's HR department or local job agent to arrange how to select the most right foreign employees to cooperate with its local manager(s) to work in overseas office(s) in team together. The international firm's HR department can only concentrate on dealing local employees issues. All foreign employees recruitment activites which will be arranged to deal from the foreign outsourcing job agent.

However, concerning foreign employee performance evaluation, reward management, training arrangement , benefits , promotion department's issues which will be dealed from the international firm's itself HR department. The foreign outsourcing staffing selection job agent is one assistant role. It only needs to gather all foreign outsourcing employee individual file of productivities record, performance reward record, clients complaining record, salary level record to let the department managers to know. Then all these foreign employee individual personal record information will be sent to the international firm's HR department to review at every year end. This international firm's HR department will enquire every overseas branch offices' deparment managers recommendation about every foreign employee individual performance as well as it will follow up all these foreign employee personnel data record to evaluate whether whom can be promoted or dismissed or increased salary level, or provided more benefit, or none change to the foreign employee. Hence, every foreign department manager's duty will need to supervise every foreign employee team performance to evaluate whether which is efficient or non-efficient team in order to decide whom foreign employee ought need to be promoted or dismissed or increased salary or trained to raise skills or working knowledge.

In conclusion, it is better to any international firms to find foreign outsourcing staff selecting job suitable foreign employees to do the positions in foreign offices. It can help itself HR department to share workload definitely.

● Outsourcing HR advantages and disadvantges

Some large organizations will choose to outsource their some HR tasks from outsourcing HR specialists to help them to do some HR related tasks, e.g. selection, performance, reward, management etc. consultant tasks. Hence, these outsourcing HR specialist will be the firm's consultant role. It needs to give recommendation whether how it ought follow which performance management method is the suitable to achieve to evaluate every employee individual performance more accurate in order to decide the employee ought need to be promoted or raised salary level, or it ought how to choose reward or benefit management plan to achieve the most reasonable and the most attractive award policy to compensate to every employee and benefit in order to let its award is fair to every need.

It brings these questions: How does tht firm decide whether it ought seek outsourcing HR specialists to live recommendation need ? Whether which kinds of HR related tasks, it ought choose outsource to HR specialists to replace its HR department's some tasks?

Outside resourcing or outsourcing of HR tasks is seem by manay as a future trend, which brings many benefits to the partners between the HR specialist partner and the outsourcing client. So, in long term beneficial cooperation relationship , the HR specialist will be one partner role to its outsoucing HR client. Because it hopes it can contribute to find its HR recommendation service, it will spend more time and effort to concentrate on gathering datas concern the firm's every employee performance evaluation method data or /and reward management method data whether they both are the best HR strategies to evaluate every employee performance fairly and give reward to every one fairly. If it found a few HR problems appear, due to demanding requirement of clients, or its clients feel lack of experience leading to solve HR difficulties in selecting which kinds of selection, performance evaluation, reward and beneficial methods are the best suitable to satisfy employee individual need. It will need to spend time and effort to compare different kinds of performance evaluation and award and beneficial methods to decide whether which one is the best suitable method to be used for their organizations' reward and performance strategies.

Wilcocks, Fitzgerald, (1993) explained the following options for HR outsourcing given the multiple criteria of classification as below:

(1) The proportion of HR outsourcing , total selective, partical.

(2) Outsourcing can be applied in human strategy, project development management and service management.

(3) The outsourcing contract can be general, transitional or of an economic

process.

(4) The type of outsourcing relationships can be described as: one provider -one customer , one supplier more customers, some vendors , a or several vendors, more customers.

(5) The period of outsourcing can be on long term or short term.

(6) Location of the supplier is local, international, offshore and regional (near shore) , closer to the customer.

The components of an HR outsourcing strategy needs to include these elements to bring these benefits from one human resources outsourcing company. They include: on benefit administration aspect, employee insurance plans arrangement, e.g. health, dental, pension, personnel files ; on HR management aspect, HR consulting, employee communication, counsel for employee issues, training arrangement, interview arrangement; on employment law aspect, solving employee labour somplaints, dealing labour union and employee individual benefits argument issues. However, HR outsourcing also brings disadvantages to organizations. If the HR outsourcing specialist changes high service fee. It will bring high cost to the outsoucing firm. When, it can not achieve to reduce HR employement costs, improve employee individual performance, raise efficient productivities.

So, the HR outsourcing firms ought to choose some simple HR tasks to attempt to examine the first choice of outsourcing HR specialist's effort, if it feels its service performance is not achieve its need. Then, it won't lose too much service fee. It can choose another outsourcing HR specialist to replace it. The outsourcing HR specialists' service may include as below:

Outsourcing to improve overall cost and predictability of employee benefits. So, the outsourcing HR specialist needs to maintain the quality, options and features of suitable employee benefits. They include health care coverage, e.g. medial , dental choice health care flexible spending planning arrangement, commuter benefit life insurance and personal accident insurance, short term and long term disability insurance choice arrangement.

Outsourcing to reduce payroll and adminitration burdens. So the outsourcing HR specialist needs to bring a benefit to the HR outsourcing client from a decrease in time spending with payroll processing and maintaining wage records, receivable reliable assistance with tasks such as: payroll processing that export pay check preparation and delivery.

Assistance with employer-related laws and regulation , e.g. administister people in accordance with the country's labour law, and help to the outsourcing HR firm client properly report salary tax to government administer unemployment claims.

Helping the HR outsoucing client to reduce liability , such as solving any employee individual complaint with HR related law and dealing workers' compensation cliams support.

Helping the HR outsourcing client to access to seasoned HR professional. It employs knowledgeable professionals who specialize in HR and can be trusted to handle issues in timely and thorough manner, including: employee liability awareness training, employee relations support, employee claiming investigation and mediation.

Helping the HR outsourcing client to freedom to focus on core business issues, e.g. giving recommendation how to improve employee performance, raising productivities growthm, avoiding reduce non-related employee essential cost.

● HR related cost reduction aim

In fact , many organizations choose HR outsouring. Their main aim is cost HR relation reduction. They hope outsourcing HR specialist can help them to give the best HR cost redicing recommendation, e.g. how to improve employee performance and raise productive efficiency, how to reduce employee adsenteeism number, how to reduce employee turnover leaving number, how to raise employee individual engagement, how to apply interview method to select the best employees to fo any low , middle and high level positions , how to attract talent applicants to choose to apply their organizations' any positions, how to raise employee morale. All these cost will be HR related cost, when the organization decides to seek one outsourcing HR specialist to help them to implement any HR strategies effectively.

Hence, such one international firm which needs to set up office in overseas. It can outsources one overseas HR specialist to give recommendation and help it how to select the foreign country's the best quality of employees to serve its foreign organization, how to arrange the most suitable and the most attractive reward and welfare benefit to attract foreign employees to work for its foreign organization, how to select the best performance evaluation methods to measure every foreign employee individual performance more accurate in order to judge whom has the actual effort to be promoted to do complex jobs more accurate. Because when one international firm needs to enter overseas market to sell its products or provide service, it must not familiarize the foreign country(countries) market, it must need the foreign country's HR specialist to give its recommendation how to implement its HR strategy to adapt the overseas country (countries) employees reward, welfare etc. needs. In conclusion, whether the organization needs outsourcing HR specialist to help it to implement HR strategy. It depends on the firm familiarizes the foreign country's people whether what are their actual needs in order to attract talents to choose to apply the organization's any kinds of positions. So, in this suitation, the international firm ought choose to find one foreign outsourcing HR specialist to help it to implement any HR related strategies which is better than implementing the foreign country's HR strategies from itself. Unless the international firm familiarizes the foreign country's labour market whether whom like overseas employers can provide what award and welfare in order to attract the foreign country / countries talent applicants to choose to serve its organization. Then, it can implement HR strategy to the foreign country's market from itself.

reference
Wilcocks, L. Fitzgerald, G., "market as opportunity? case studies in outsourcing information technology and services." , Journal of strategic information systems, vol. 2 no 3. 1993 pp. 201-217

Engagement Strategy solves
wood Medical Centre organization international different culture difficult cooperation problemHill
● How and why can engagement strategy solve medical organizational departments difficult culture cooperate problem ?
Organizational cultures and subcultures will influence Hill wood Medical Centre organizational performance and commitments. The subcultures may take precedence over the organizational culture for individual employees and thus gain their commitment. Hill wood medical centre can therefore focus on the relationships of both organizational culture and subcultures to satisfy staffs need to serve patients in happy work environment. Organizational culture includes leadership style and job satisfactory measurement. Hence, employees' commitment was examined in relation to the level of consent to and conflict with managerial strategy. Although, managerial strategy is not the same as leadership, the attributes and skills required in leadership could be seen as an essential part of managerial strategy. Organization culture(s) has (have) a causal modelling

approach to examine the determinants of organizational commitment and labour turnover. Organization culture(s) can include a variety of variables , e.g. age, pre-employment expectations, perceived job characteristics and the consideration of leadership style, which all influence organizational commitment indirectly via effects on job satisfaction. I supposed that Hill Wood Medical Centre existed relationship of organizational culture and subcultures to influence staffs feel satisfactory and commitment. Also of interest is the relationship of these variables with leadership style, job satisfaction and subject characteristics, such as age, level of education to its staffs in this hospital.

In Hill Wood Medical Centre organization, its organizational culture was the hospital cultures and subcultures which refer to the culture of the wards or work units or operation rooms to every department staff commitments refer to nurses team and medical service chief medical officer team and surgeons team and administrative department etc their different departments' individual staff's commitments. There is a culture relationship between this medical centre organization commitments and it was measured with administration department and operating rooms and wards department etc different departments' subcultures as well as surgeons and nurses and doctors and administration staffs etc different teams' subcultures. More specifically, it is expected that such as Hill Wood Medical Centre organizational culture could be more supportive and innovative to its different departments, such as
wards and surgeons operating rooms and administrative office etc different departments subcultures.

Thus, I believe there is a strong relationship between this medical centre organizational cultures and subcultures and commitment and characteristics of
this organizational overall culture, such as corporate values and beliefs commitments and performance to Hill Wood Medical Centre organization. However, I think this medical centre's bureaucratic work practices organizational cultures often result in negative employee commitment due to its supportive work
environment could not result in greater commitment and involvement among employees. For example, these different departments needed to met Sharon Lawson, administrator of Hill Wood Medical Centre to discuss how to solve their departments problems in their meetings in that day, but Sharon Lawson could not had any suggestions in these meeting in that day.

It seemed that this medical centre had negative culture and subcultures to get negative results due to who needed to spend time to wait Sharon to meet them and the administrator could not give any suggestions to solve their department problems on that day. Such as Holly from state health department told Sharon the general inspection needed to be improved, e.g. kitchen needed cleanliness and inspectors felt this medical centre needed to allow patients access to drug supplies, but this state health department representative had requested inspection before six months and Helen controller asked Sharon about

the new computer hardware who requested six months ago and Helen told Sharon who needed it now for billing efficiency to office use, but Sharon decided to make request to board for computer hardware purchase next meeting and some surgeons were drunk to work in operating rooms, who caused danger to patient's life to cause some patients complained these surgeons, but Sharon did not solve whose complaints at that day immediately and medical staffs were discussing why the medical centre had not purchased one upgraded piece of standard diagnostic equipment used in body scanning $700,000 cost, but Sharon had not enquired whose reasons clearly to decide to buy the equipment next year, but doctors did not understand why Sharon could not purchased this year. Then the nurses agreed to give Sharon a week to investigate the situation

and attempted to resolve it and a meeting was scheduled for next week to review the situation.

Finally the medical centre's attorney needed to wait for twenty minutes to discuss about what steps were to be taken to solve with surgeons, Dr Chambers who was complained about drunk wine work in surgeon operating rooms issue, but Sharon had no more time to meet whom to discuss on that day. Hence, it seemed that this medical centre had not good culture and subcultures in its organization, such as Sharon had not enough time arrangement to meet them to discuss their departments' problems on the same day. It seemed that Hill Wood Medical Centre had no good organizational culture and subcultures to cause staffs conflicts and administration department also wasted much time to handle departments' meetings only. If Hill Wood Medical centre culture and subcultures could be changes, such as every department could attempt to discuss how to solve their problems before who met the administrator . Then I believe that who could give reasons or ideas to support their view point to persuade Sharon made final decision to shorten their meeting time. Hence, this medical centre seemed that it's subcultures and culture were negative.

I supposed that it's nurses team subcultures tended to identify more cooperation closely with different teams, such as surgeons operating rooms team, doctors team, wards team etc departments to compare the administration department. It meant nurses teams' subcultures needed often exhibit greater loyalty and commitment to these departments in the Hill wood

Medical Centre organization. Thus, it seemed that it needed better subcultures in nurses teams to share different departments' job to reduce staffs conflicts to serve patients satisfactory. However, Hill Wood Medical Centre organizational culture and subcultures could influence

staffs' job satisfaction and commitment positively or negatively due to this medical centre cultural variables could influence their feelings , such as the amount of reward, flexibility of work schedule and balance of work and home life etc. Hence, Hill Wood Medical Centre culture could cause those intrinsic factors to influence every units staffs' feelings of job satisfaction. In relation to educational level and organizational

commitment, it seemed that educational level was negatively relative to this Hill Wood Medical centre, such as it could permit surgeons were drunk to work in operating rooms often, it was danger to every patient life during surgeons were drunk to work . Hill Wood Medical Centre overall culture was from low to top level communication channel and bureaucratic work organizational culture was often in negative employee commitment, such as all departments needed to wait the administrator to arrange meeting time to solve their departments problems in the same day. However, much decisions could not get solutions from the administrator.

It seemed that this Hill Wood Medical Centre's bureaucratic organization cultures and subcultures caused Sharon had arranged more meetings on that day to influence who had not enough time to do their departments' duties on that day efficiently due to who only concentrated on handling meetings issues on that day. I think Sharon Lawson who did not know how to arrange what kinds of job duties and meetings which were more important which ought to handle on that day or what kinds of job duties and meetings which were not more important to handle on the same day. Hence, who could not get any discussion result in these meetings on that day due to Sharon, administrator had not enough time to negotiate their departments to solve problems successfully in meetings. In conclusion, this medical centre organizational cultures and subcultures seemed that which were not positive to staffs' commitments and job satisfaction. Such as its different departments needed to spend much time to wait administrator to arrange meetings to discuss their problems, but who did not make any decisions in their meetings. The administrator would influence different departments overall work efficiency and effectiveness to be poor. So, it ought need to change its organization culture and subcultures to raise its different departments' efficiency and effectiveness as soon as possible.

● suggestion engagement strategy influences to medical centre departments' staffs build kindly culture efficient cooperative method

Describe the culture or cultures at Hill wood Medical Centre ? Are these subcultures ?

How would you recommend that Sharon administrator measure effectiveness at Hill wood Medical Centre?

The medical centre performance effective evaluation meant to measure whether the degree to its overall organization was improving or deteriorating. The measurement combines quantitative and qualitative analysis and efficiency trend to get the degree of effective result. On the quantitative analyses measurement, e.g. medical errors occurrence rates ; patients medical treatment health rates. On the qualitative analysis measurement, e.g.acquiring executives who communicated a culture of quality through personal supportive polities
and investment of resources, such as the degree of diagnostic equipments effectiveness, the degree of staff quality improvement and the degree of health information technological
effectiveness and the degree of every patient's service satisfaction etc. Performance measurement effectiveness is well established throughout medical and health care industry, of which include the core areas of finance, operations, clinical care and information technology services as below:

Finance is an organization often measures the efficiency of its accounts receivable, i.e. timely collection of payment for services rendered, such as this Hill Wood medical centre can collect how much payment for services from patients per week and it earns how much profit or loss per week. Operating is an organization needs the lengths of time to take for a patient to receive an appointment in the practice or measures individual patient whose satisfaction with the care received, such as the satisfactory degree of Hill Wood Medical Centre every patient
how who feel to every doctor, physician, surgeon and nurse whose service performance and personal attitude to whom.

Clinical care is an organization measures how often care is delivered in accordance with evidence based guidelines or how effective that care is in improving every patient outcome,
such as whether Hill Wood medical centre had how many doctor and surgeon and physician and nurse numbers who could treat every patient to be health to satisfy who don't feel sick or
hurt again after who left this hospital. Information technology is an organization widely integrated into health care settings to support for performance measurement, such as whether Hill Wood medical centre needed to buy how many diagnostic equipments to use to body scanning for surgeons or needed to buy how many computers to office to use to achieve the best performance.

This Hill Wood medical centre needed these processes to measure its quantified numbers to a health care service provided to on behalf of or by a patient that was needed on scientific evidence of efficiency or effectiveness, so it could quantify a specific system, e.g. getting a test done or a
service performed and it's outcome could measure to quantify every patient's health status resulting from its nurses and doctors and surgeons and physicians whose health care. Thus, in the clinical area, Hill Wood medical centre could measure every patient outcome to compare to every care standard, such as every patient's test value to measure effectiveness. Measurement effectiveness is central to the concept of this Hill Wood medical centre quality improvement, it provides a
mean to define what medical centres or hospitals actually do and to compare that with the original targets in order to identify opportunities for improvement. On clinical care and operational measure aspect:

Hill Wood medical centre ought to establish standardized and systematic procedures for problem solving to able to test and implement major practice changes. Such as clinical
guidelines or care maps for specific conditions or procedures, department specific quality plans with short and long term goals, improved educational and training materials for clinical staff error reduction, hand washing and infection prevention, education materials for patients regarding full prevention, information technology that reduced medication errors and improved data collection etc these changes. To decide whether how much change criteria it ought need to change it's measurement effectiveness was depending on the nature of the
change and the rate of acceptance and adoption of staff. It aimed to

resistance to change in culture from surgeons and physicians and nurses and doctors; measured how much limited

resources were available to use or maintain quality related equipment investment, such as office equipments or operational rooms diagnostic equipments of numbers as well as

whether how to make the patient complaint numbers to be reduced to achieve zero tolerance to any staffs as well as whether departmental quality plans could achieve special goals effectiveness measurement as well as whether training could be achieve continuous quality improvement to staffs measure

effectiveness as well as organizational structure change could be raised staffs service performance efficiently, such as whether creation was needed on service quality and addition staff and responsibilities were needed for quality improvement

as well as whether patient care redesign and more training was needed for aides and multi disciplinary leadership teams change. Establishing organizational culture and subcultures of service quality measurement effectiveness aspect as below:

. Setting how long time to achieve short term and long term attainable goals and celebrated successes to individual staff and individual units involved in reaching their goals.

. Keeping the individual unit staff involved in problem identification and problem solving time spending. It aimed to raise everyone to feel much valuing expecting all to participate

to solve any problems in the most shorten time.

On finance and information technology measure effective aspect:

Effective organizational culture and subculture change could encourage every unit leader and peers to be patient, but recognized that changing took time and continuing to keep quality improvement to measure whether it needed how much time to balance quality and financial goals and considering investments, such as how many equipment numbers were needed to buy to provide to office and operational room units to use to raise office productive efficiency and effectiveness as well as operational rooms service efficiency and effectiveness to measure to achieve quality improvement from a short and long term perspective to this Hill Wood medical centre. It aimed to evaluate whether new policies were bringing equipment into

operating rooms or office to use was needed or was not needed .

I recommend Sharon, administrator needed to indicate these qualitative performance effectiveness measurement questions included:

.What barriers did this medical centre face in implementing the strategies or achieving success?

.Did it overcome those obstacles and if so, how?

In conclusion, to measure effectiveness of this medical centre whether how it could achieve quality improvement for success. I recommend Sharon, administrator needed to consider what should be the indicators to include implementation of aggressive quality targets for performance indicators as well as how to decide tightening of recruitment and standards and enhanced respect for all staffs in enhancement of quality improvement processes to shorten time to solve problems in

efficient manner and hoped to decide new investments in quality related information technology combined with the number of staffs input numbers efficiently and effectively.

Thus, the four core areas of performance measurement was one quality improvement models of high performing effective measurement to Hill Wood Medical Centre.

What do you think some of the effectiveness criteria might be?

I think some outcomes of effectiveness criteria to this Hill Wood medical centre, it might be the practice changes appeared to have resulted in improved outcomes for patients. In

addition to major improvements in the combination quality measures which based on morality, morbidity and complication rates, such as below:

Process/ operations effectiveness criteria: faster receipt of test result, faster patient flow, easier and more efficient data sharing and recording, fewer medication errors. So, I think it could measure the doctors and nurses and surgeons and physicians who serve to every patient's performance whether what effectiveness criteria to these staffs from their every serving patients' satisfactory level. Health related effectiveness criteria: calculate the reductions in morality rates, e.g. the surgeon reducing numbers were drunk to work in operational rooms every month and the patient health numbers every month.

Work environment and reputation effectiveness criteria: increase in patients satisfaction and staff satisfaction numbers and morale improved status numbers every month in this medical centre. If it could increase the numbers of patients satisfaction and staff satisfaction and morale improved status numbers, it would have greater ability to improve service quality to surgeons and doctors and nurses in this medical centre.

Bottom line effectiveness criteria: the effective measurement of decreasing or increasing costs per medical centre units and length of stay for certain conditions and increased or

decreased patients admission numbers and market share numbers every month. I think it lacked enough equipments for office to use and diagnostic equipments numbers were needed to be upgraded to use in body scanning because the departments leaders needed to met to Sharon, administrator to permit to buy those equipments urgently. It seemed this medical centre service effectiveness criteria would be poor due to there was not enough equipments to provide to these units to use possibly. Hence, if this medical centre could raised the quantitative and qualitative effectiveness criteria as above, it would change positive outcomes to motivate these units doctors, surgeons, nurses, physicians and administrative individual team leaders and their colleagues to strengthen the service quality improvement process to this Hill Wood medical centre. However, I think this Hill Wood medical centre performance was poor from the above

effectiveness criteria analysis. Performance must be defined in relative to explicit goals reflecting the values of various stakeholders.

On conclusion, when the international medical center can have one excellent engagement strategy, it can solve international medical staffs whose cooperative challenges more easily. This medical centre internal stakeholders were

such as patients, doctors, nurses, surgeons, physicians etc and external stakeholders were patients, debtors, banks, Government shareholders etc. This medical centre performance might be defined according to the achievement of specific targets of

either clinic to patient services or internal departmental operations. Targets might relate to traditional hospital functions, such as health treatment, care and rehabilitation as well as administration, ambulatory patient delivered services and health care networks. Following this medical centre evidences which indicated the poor performance of effectiveness criteria, such as Sharon, administrator lacked enough time to meet some department leaders to help them to solve problems successfully on that day, so it caused who needed to make another

meetings to discuss their problems again. It seemed the administrator wasted their time to do other important duties on that day efficiently and effectively. I think Sharon, administrator was not one effective administrator in this medical centre. If who could not change whose management attitude to co-operate with other department managers(leaders), then who could cause poor subcultures to different departments to build to this medical centre overall organization culture and who also influenced other department performed ineffective and inefficient results due to Sharon, administrator who did not know how to arrange time to meet them everyone efficiently.

In conclusion, I think if this medical centre hoped to reduce doctors and nurses and surgeons and physicians and administrations etc staffs frequently conflict and maximized work effectiveness of its departments. Sharon administrator had responsibility to change whose personal work attitude to adapt their subcultures to co-operate with different departments. Otherwise, this medical centre would not be maximize effectiveness and would increase staffs conflicts to cause staff turnover numbers to be increased seriously.